For Bruce, with love

Love &
Trouble

Memoirs of a
Former Wild Girl

Claire Dederer

TINDER
PRESS

First published by Alfred A. Knopf, USA

First published in Great Britain in 2017 by Tinder Press
An imprint of HEADLINE PUBLISHING GROUP

This edition published in 2018 by Tinder Press
An imprint of HEADLINE PUBLISHING GROUP

1

Cataloguing in Publication Data is available from the British Library

Trade Paperback ISBN 978 1 4722 3117 8

Offset in 11/16 pt Celeste by Jouve (UK), Milton Keynes

Printed and bound in Great Britain by Clays Ltd, St Ives plc

Headline's policy is to use papers that are natural, renewable and recyclable
products and made from wood grown in well-managed forests and other
controlled sources. The logging and manufacturing processes are expected
to conform to the environmental regulations of the country of origin.

HEADLINE PUBLISHING GROUP
An Hachette UK Company
Carmelite House
50 Victoria Embankment
London EC4Y 0DZ

www.tinderpress.co.uk
www.headline.co.uk
www.hachette.co.uk

Contents

CONTENTS

You, Now

You did everything right!

You made some friends you could count on. You got a job. You found a mate, a really nice one, and you bought a house and had kids. You didn't even think about it that much, you just did it. You worked really hard, all the time. You were a faithful wife and, it's okay to say it out loud, an above-average mom, and you dressed cute but not too cute. You were a little afraid. You were a lot afraid. You could feel your chaotic past behind you. You could hear the girl you were, a disastrous pirate slut of a girl, breathing down your neck. You wanted nothing to do with her. But sometimes late at night, while the babies and the husband were asleep, you drank Maker's Mark in your living room, even though you were still breastfeeding, and you listened to music alone in the dark, and that girl came closer and closer until you turned off the music and went to your marital bed and slept your dreamless, drunken sleep. You woke up and your teeth felt like nervy stubs from all the grinding. You had a headache that lived inside your teeth.

You accumulated this life over a decade, maybe two. Like a midden, or the nest of a bowerbird, or a creepy shut-in's collection of nail clippings. Anyway, it all piled up, accreted, because that was the way you wanted it. You are the kind of person who gets what she wants. You *wanted* to accumulate this beautiful life, a life that—for all its beauty—ignored the person you'd been. You worked your ass off getting here.

You moved to the country, or that's what you called it. Just because you take a ferry to get there and you have farmers for neighbors, that doesn't make it the country. It's just very, very picturesque suburbs. In the fake country, there was all the nature you craved. You had woods in your new backyard and a badminton lawn and a poorly kept garden that you described to yourself as romantically overgrown. Also, the schools were terrific. The house you bought was a bit bigger so your daughter and son didn't have to share a bedroom, even though it's great for kids to share a bedroom, but maybe a little uncomfortable as they get older. You bought a nice new couch, because toddlers left the old one as stained with shit and vomit and blood as the backseat of Travis Bickle's taxi. You had orthodontia for the children, who got really large, really fast. In your safe, pretty house in the alleged country, across the water from the city where you grew up, you mostly forgot about the girl you were, the lost soul. She was such a clueless bitch, you didn't really want to think about her anyway. Maybe you conjured her at parties with new friends, parents from your kids' school who laughed, politely, at your crazy stories. You woke up embarrassed the next morning.

And then one day it's as if a switch is flipped. This day comes in April 2011, the spring you are forty-four years old. You don't know it yet, but on this day, your season in hell has begun. You stumble out of bed. Your husband, a journalist, is headed somewhere far away on assignment, but before he leaves he brings you coffee in bed and then yells up the stairs at your children. You rise and go into the kitchen, lean dizzily against the counter, and watch them come in their multitudes. Well, there are only two of them, but they seem like more in the morning.

Your daughter, solemn and big-eyed and possessed of a slyly wicked sense of humor, is twelve; just around the age you were when you started going off the rails. Does her twelve-ness fill you with anxiety? If so, you're not quite admitting it to yourself. She grows more beautiful every day, even as you grow homelier, no matter how many *chaturangas* you perform. A friend discovered, at the health food store on your island, something called emu oil. As far as you can tell from the gnomic description on the tiny bottle, it appears to be secreted from the glands of emus. Which glands? Unknown. Whatever, it makes you and all the other ladies in your neighborhood look *great*. Glowy. Everyone goes for it in a big way for a month or so, but after a while it just seems too gross. Meanwhile your daughter appears to be coolly lit from within by some tiny inner moon. Does her comparative glowiness make you feel that your own mortality, your own youth, is drawing inexorably to a close? Again, not in any way you care to admit.

Your son, for now, is a simpler matter: nine years old, cherubic, and uncomplicatedly loving and gleefully loud. And here they come, every morning, with their crazed hair and vacant eyes. They are like sleep-hot monsters who need to have the wildness of dreaming smoothed and fed and nagged out of them.

Your husband is picking up his suitcase and heading out the door and the kids are looking for their shoes. Because from the time they're born until they're eighteen, there will be one constant: lost shoes.

Your life is relentlessly communal. You are necessary, in every conceivable way. This is how you wanted it to be. Blessedly alone at last, you sit down at your computer to work on an overdue article. Your focus is shitty. Through the open window you hear the call of a spotted towhee, which sounds *exactly* like the Austin Powers theme song. The spring air is the very gas of nostalgia. It reminds you of schoolrooms, of wanting to flee your desk, of the escape artist you used to be. As you sit there, you find that all of a sudden you can't stop thinking about her, the girl you were.

The thing is, you don't really remember her that well, because you've spent so long trying to block her out. You suddenly want evidence of her existence. You go down into the basement, as one in a trance, and start rummaging through boxes. You kneel penitent-like on the cold cement floor, looking for her.

Letters are easy to come by. There are boxes full of them. They overflow plastic bags, they fall out of books like flat fledging birds. Letters were the way you and your friends found one another when you were young; you stuffed your little all into an envelope and dropped it in the box and waited. Friendships were kept alive for years in this manner. Letters weren't rare and precious; they were the papery stuff of life, or emotional life anyway, and that's really the only life you cared about when you were young.

You stack the letters neatly in a pile and you keep looking, rooting around like a truffle pig. Photos are a little scarcer; people didn't use to take photos for everyday entertainment. When you were young, seeing a photo of yourself was an event. Oh my god, you'd think, I'm backward! Because of course you only ever saw your mirror image, which was a lying bastard.

Your diaries, which are a multivolume situation, prove strangely elusive. They aren't all stored together. Each move from house to house has scattered them into different boxes. It's as though you've hidden yourself from yourself. You begin to tear through boxes. You find a diary crammed into a carton of old concert T-shirts, T-shirts that themselves could be read as a diary: the Rolling Stones's *Tattoo You* tour, Beat Happening, Died Pretty, the Melvins, the Presidents of the United States of America. You find another diary wedged between layers of your children's baby clothes, which you are saving because you are a sap; you find three mixed up with books from college by people like Clifford Geertz and Michel Foucault. Whenever your hand falls on one of these diaries, you feel a whoosh of luck. It is the book you most want to read.

You haul all this stuff out to your backyard studio, a tiny building a few necessary yards from your house. This is where you come to while away the hours by yourself, avoiding your family, like one of those emotionally withholding British husbands who spend their days in the shed at the bottom of the garden, pursuing who knows what obsession: Porn? Philately? You, on the other hand, come out here to write and cry. It's luxurious to have a little house where you can go to weep, though your actual surroundings are pretty humble: salvaged windows, plywood floor, spare furnishings. You give an experimental little sniff and smell what is unmistakably an animal tang. There's a nest of raccoons living under the shed.

You spend too much time out here; it's one of your escape hatches. Without admitting it, you've been building a little collection of these over the last few months—ever since around the time you turned forty-four. Maybe they're starting to get out of hand. You've always been close with your best friend, Victoria, but suddenly you're on the phone every day, like lovers: "I had tuna fish for lunch." "I cried instead of eating lunch." You're both married to men who are smart and loving and tall and funny. Even so, you and she travel together like a couple. Why do you leave these excellent men at home? You're not sure exactly. It has something to do with valves; with escaping pressure. Anyway, she joins you on book tour and you accompany her to openings (she's an artist); in all instances you drink too much. Speaking of lovahs, you have a slew of inappropriate e-mail friendships with men. They're not quite romantic but you shouldn't have to say that. Even sex with your husband, which has always been a point of connection, a relief, a release, has become an escape hatch, infused with the outsiders who are starting to cluster in your imagination. You don't quite imagine them when you're fucking your husband; except you do, actually. Sex is changing and becoming dirty again, just now when you are getting truly old and bits of you are lumpy that ought to be smooth. You find yourself over his knee, or with parts of him in your mouth, and you want to sort of rub your eyes and say: How'd we end up *here*? You know it's not this way for all women. For every person like you, with this crazed gleam in your eye, there're three other women who say they'd be happy doing it once a month, or less; they'd be happy with just a cuddle. You get it. You know how they feel. You've felt that way yourself. But not now. Now you feel like this: Jesus Christ, we're all going to die! Get it while you can, you morons!

Most surprising of all—for a woman like you, a woman who's been keeping her shit at least somewhat together lo these many years—is your diminishing sanity, your diminishing energy, your diminishing competence. A new inertia has overcome you. Once upon a time, you used to come out to your office and work hard, beavering away at your current article. Since you published your first book, though, you find work more difficult than ever. You're not sure why this is. Many people said nice things, in print and elsewhere, when your book came out, but like a real writer you care only about the mean stuff, the indignities. You received a savage e-mail from a mentor and former editor of yours, who told you the book was so unreadable she had to stop midway through. She sent what she called "a note, maybe a goodbye." That left a mark, bigger than you care to admit. You are shaken and insecure, and simultaneously enervated.

So you sit there in your office, staring out the window at the fuchsia that for some reason no longer blooms. You are too enervated to prune it back to fecundity. You're like a windup toy that can't get wound. You find yourself able to achieve gape-mouthed catatonia, a state you haven't known in decades. Working mothers of very young children are not allowed catatonia; it's a country they can't get a visa to. Proud Catatonia, flying the flag of idleness and melancholy. You find yourself suddenly not just wanting to do nothing but somehow *needing* to do nothing.

Maybe a woman's version of a midlife crisis involves *stopping doing stuff*?

It's not like stopping doing stuff is new to you. You were basically non-utile for many years, from about age thirteen to age twenty-three, and were beloved in spite of this undeniable fact, or maybe even because of it. You did nothing, and it was more than enough. Then you decided you wanted to be valued for what you could do—writing, mothering, housekeeping, editing, teaching, gardening, cooking—and you worked hard at acquiring those skills. And now you've gotten your wish: You are loved for your usefulness. Is it an achievement or a curse? You and your husband's love for each other is based on profound reciprocity: What can you do for me? What can I do for you? This is considered a healthy marriage; you think about each other's needs. You cover the bases. He does money; you do food. Like that.

The two of you pass the big tests: You still talk; you still fuck. But sometimes you ruefully recall Ethan Hawke's character in *Before Sunset,* when he describes his marriage: "I feel like I'm running a small nursery with someone I used to date." You resent the fact that you've been forced to relate to Ethan Hawke. Of all people. And anyway of course it's worth it. Your family isn't some kind of chore, or even some kind of mere consolation, though it's both those things as well. It's the whole deal, the great love, the thing in this life that was supposed to happen to you. Even so, your family members certainly require a lot of work. From you. And so sometimes you wish you could be loved just for being. You find yourself yearning to stop. Every-thing. Doing nothing is suddenly on the agenda in a big way. You like nothing so much that you occasionally lie in bed all day and think about nothing. (This is not optimal, financially speaking, and your waning earnings are not doing a lot to make you popular with your husband.) You have a lot of nothing to think about, for the first time in a long time. You are interested in nothing.

Just now you are interested in this, though. This basement evidentiary material. There in your studio, you lay out the photos, the letters, the diaries, and read them, and look at them. They look totally fabulous, exercises in superfluous beauty. The letters are covered with tiny drawings and declarations of love and unnecessary curlicues. The photos are silly and gorgeous and everyone looks skinnier (their bodies) but at the same time chubbier (their faces) than they do now. The diaries are intricate woolgatherings, collections of meandering self-thought, involuted as a vulva, spiraling as a conch shell, thought and self making a net or a trap. And there she is. That horrible girl.

June 4, 1979, age twelve

I wonder if these thoughts of death will ever leave my mind. I wonder what love is like.

2

A Geography of Crying

I laid all the diaries out in a line on my desk and tentatively peeked inside them. They made me feel ridiculously maudlin. I was like Brian Wilson, doing my sighing and my crying, laughing at yesterday, in my room. In fact, all the women were crying. Our husbands and boyfriends and partners thought it was self-pity. Maybe it was. They said it was self-indulgent and sort of bratty. Probably so. And yet we went on crying. We didn't know why. All the women were crying, but we didn't cry everywhere. We didn't cry at our children's school; or at our regular grocery store, where the checkers knew us; or at work, or at least at meetings at work. We stored our tears up and then turned them on, faucet-like, when the place was right.

There were certain places that seemed to give rise to tears, places that were like fissures in the emotional earth that made geysering possible or even probable. Seattle is not a big city for crying. Seattle, in fact, is famously emotionally stoppered. There are many theories as to why this is the case; some say it's because of our dominant genetic and cultural heritages: Norwegian and Japanese. Whatever the reason, Seattle is a place where you are not supposed to emote. You are supposed to endure. In Seattle, where rain and traffic are two snakes twining, choking the body of the city, forbearance is an art. We don't cry, we just put on more Gore-Tex or maybe use the driving time of our commute to listen to a self-improvement book on tape. Though "driving" is a strong word for what happens when you get into a car in Seattle.

And yet suddenly there were these crying hot spots, where our stoppered emotions flowed, whether we liked it or not.

J and I were having coffee at a cozy little bakery on Queen Anne Hill. We were ravenous; we had forgotten to eat today. Were both good cooks, better than good. If you're not a good cook by the time you're our age it's a serious character defect, and it means something bad, something ungenerous, about your personality. Sorry to break the news. Anyway, we could cook just fine, but somehow we'd forgotten how to eat. Food was wearisome. We'd been dealing with food, planning it buying it growing it storing it cooking it serving it, for years, for decades now. By the time it was our moment to eat, we were sick of the sight of it. Fuck food.

Food looked a little better, though, when it wasn't inside our houses. We bought salads with meat in them because we knew we needed protein—it was as if we were our own toddlers. The way I remembered it, that was the main objective with toddlers: the posting of protein into them.

Once we had our meats and greens, we found a little table. I ended up facing east (in Seattle, I always, always know the direction I am facing, whether cardinal or ordinal, even indoors). I had sat at this same table, in this same position with J before, and always there were tears. It was as though the table was making her cry, like the mean kid on the playground.

J was exactly my age, a newish friend. She and her husband were separating after twenty-plus years of marriage and four children. This morning they went to the marriage counselor.

"He"—J was referring to her husband and starting to leak hard—"said he welcomed the break. And Adrian"—now she was referring to the shrink—"*let* him. Adrian just sat there and let him say all this stuff *I'd* done wrong."

You might think, as I did, that this sounded exactly like therapy. But I was able to discern the outlines of my job here, and it didn't involve unhelpful realism. So I said instead the thing you say: "I know." I nodded as I said it. She nodded. Some empathetic currency had been exchanged. Why was this *knowing* so important? The truth was of course that I didn't know. It wasn't my marriage. I didn't have a fucking clue. But still I said it: "I know."

J in her sobbing, her tearfulness, her out-of-controlness, felt unknown, perhaps most of all to herself. Who was this weeping woman? she wondered. Where did she come from? When I said "I know," I was really saying: "I know you." In other words: "You are still J. I recognize you. You're still the person you were before all this fucking crying started."

J gave a mighty sniff and squeezed my hand. "Thank you, sweetie." She was always thoughtful. We took a break for a moment in the midst of the crying and the "I know"–saying, the way you pause in the middle of an especially long bout of sex or jogging. We noticed a very fat baby sitting nearby on the lap of his pretty young mother. We cooed out loud, like the crones we were. (In most societies in the history of the, you know, world, we'd have been grandmothers by now.) The young mother looked a little nervous. Was this going to happen to her? The erosion of decorum, the simplemindedness, the tide of weeping? Not to mention the physical decay? Yes.

All the women were crying, but the first crier, the last crier, the most important crier would always be Victoria. The place Victoria cried was inside my phone. Every day.

She called as I was taking my lunchtime walk. I often found myself crying as I strode along the forest path. It used to be a place of serenity; now it threatened me with possible dampness. We were discussing her upcoming show at the Seattle Art Museum, about which she harbored a deep ambivalence, the ambivalence that shadowed, it seemed, every move of the mid-career artist, and here came the tears. Vic's brain never shut off, and her standards were sky-high, and this was what made her great, and it also wasn't the easiest way to live.

"I'm sorry." She sniffed.

"I know."

Her tears came to me from a star somewhere, or however iPhones talk to each other.

Even in public, the women wept unrestrainedly and loudly. Not because they lacked social skills or because they were emotional exhibitionists. They cried like this because they'd been crying for so many months now that it just came real natural to them. Crying was simply what they did when confronted with a sympathetic face and perhaps a question of probing acuity such as "How are you doing?"

A was doing that kind of crying right now. She was a spectacle. We were on a walk around the crest of Queen Anne Hill, not far from where J and I liked to go for coffee. Clearly there was a largish crack in Seattle's emotional stability on and around Queen Anne. The early-spring air smelled of *Daphne odora*. We were the kind of women who know stuff like that, in Latin, yet. A lived in L.A., and she was passing through town on her way to a writer's retreat.

A and I were on a crying loop, circling the hilltop. We marched like anchorites around the neighborhood and A cried extravagantly. Where J leaked, A stormed, all elbows and knees, raging around the crying loop like she was getting in a workout.

A was a person of tomboyish glamour and people watched us as we went.

"Bastards!" she railed, enumerating the sins of her hard-hearted ex-lover. It was the usual boring sociopath litany; it was just that A hadn't encountered it, I hadn't encountered it, since we were in our twenties. It was intolerable, and yet she was tolerating it. But only through this lavish crying.

"I knew this was going to happen!" she said. I wasn't sure what she was talking about, but that was okay. She was feeling betrayed in general. We all were, even though we weren't sure exactly why.

Not safe: my upstairs hallway, cozy, rain hitting the metal roof. I was folding laundry when the phone rang. It was Vic. I tucked her between my shoulder and my ear—she got mad if I put her on speakerphone. In fact she would have preferred I sat still while I talked to her and just *focused.*

"Are you doing chores?" she asked.

"No!" I said, folding a pair of Willie's underpants.

We started to talk about my kids, and then we were talking about our own childhoods, and here came the tears. I mean, I couldn't hear the tears exactly. It was just a very special kind of silence. It always made us laugh.

Obviously my house was a problem area; perhaps it sat on a largish breach. My friend G was visiting with her kids. We were chatting away on the porch when G received a text regarding something work-related and began, just like that, to cry. Whether from being overwhelmed or despair or hurt feelings, who knew. I'm not sure how to emphasize this enough: G *never* cried. She came from a no-nonsense blue-collar background and was the hardest-working person I had ever met, with a kind heart but also a certain gently expressed intolerance for bullshit, especially her own. And now she was crying, sobbing, tears rolling fatly down her beautiful brown cheeks. She gave her head a shake and went to the bathroom. Emerged a few minutes later. Her eyes were swollen almost shut from crying.

I opened my arms wide and she came into them.

"Was it something I said?" I asked her hair.

She shook her head. "Uh-uh."

"Do you know *what* it was?"

Another shake of the head. "Uh-uh. I don't know *what* it is."

"It might be hormones," I suggested.

"Well, who cares?" said practical G. "Who cares if it's hormones. That doesn't make it hurt less." She sloughed the tears away with the blade of her hand—even in extremis finding the most elegant, efficient way to do the job—and drew a breath. She turned from me, started again.

"I know," I said. I sounded calm. But inside I was thinking: Holy crap! If G can't stop crying, then there's no hope for the rest of us. I went inside and made her an iced coffee. It didn't taste as good as when she made it. Nothing ever tasted as good as when she made it.

The voices of the children rose from somewhere nearby. G sipped her coffee, did that thing called getting it together. Though why? Why was it so important for our children not to see us like this?

The phone rang while I was tapping away at some dumb freelance piece. A book review. I couldn't even think properly anymore. Didn't care. I looked at the caller ID, saw it was Vic, answered with glee.

We began to recount what utter bitches we'd been to our

husbands on this fine day. Vic felt guilty, while me, I was beyond guilt. I felt distant from Bruce but the distance felt like a reprieve. We had been together for fifteen years, but since we'd both always worked at home—since in fact we were *always together*—we joked we'd been married a hundred and seventy-six years in normal-people time. Except as Morrissey says, that joke wasn't funny anymore. To me. I didn't ask how it felt to him. I didn't see that this was a problem—this incuriosity about him; this hyper-focus on my own interior. I didn't see that for the last few months I'd been slowly, surely drawing a circle around myself, and the only thing to do inside the circle was, it turned out, cry. To be honest, it was kind of a sucky circle.

Soon Vic began to leak.

"I'm a dope," she said.

"I know. Me too."

Aside from my shed-office, I cried in only one place, and it was the most embarrassing place in the world: I cried at the yoga studio, where there appeared to be a serious crevasse. I liked to go to yoga in the evenings, which was like a recipe for tears. Sweat hard in a hot room for an hour or so. Then lie down on your back in the dark. Misty, your teacher, who is as sweet and earnest as a kindergarten teacher, tells you in her tender loving impersonal way to close your eyes. She turns on Krishna Das, whose all-knowing chanting is accompanied by the harmonium, easily the most tear-inducing sound ever invented by man. So there I was in my weakened state, sodium-depleted, with Misty padding around being wonderful and Krishna Das and his fuck-ing harmonium. It was more than I could deal with. I cried help-lessly. I cried for everything I couldn't have in my good life: freedom and carelessness and some kind of undefined, perfect love that hadn't found me yet and never would. For the way I failed the people in my life. For my children and their unknown futures. For my crumbling, aging body. For failed writing. I sobbed and Krishna Das didn't say "I know." He said "Hare Krishna, Hare Rama." Which was not the same thing *at all*.

The possibility of stopping crying seemed distant. But I had to stop, because class would end and the crying would have to end with it. I couldn't walk out of the studio sniveling. I lived in a small town. My business was everyone's business. Also, I was the lady who wrote that yoga book and it wouldn't do for me to be seen bawling my head off at yoga. Every day.

That was why, maybe, this was the place where for me the membrane between the regular world and the crying world grew thin and I crossed over with my whole body. Because I knew I must get it together. We rolled onto our right sides and I wiped my tears away with my T-shirt.

Every once in a while, for a treat, I got to see Vic and we cried in person. We shouldn't have been crying. We'd both had a good year. She had a nice life with her husband in North Seattle. I had a nice life with my husband and children on my island a ferry ride away. Even so, we felt happy only when we were together and could be as sad as we really were. We usually did our crying-walking along Lake Union's industrial edge, near Vic's studio, which was about to be torn down. Gentrification had chased her out of three studios already in its relentless, personal-seeming quest to render soulless our entire city. We liked the desolation of this still-unsung, still-shabby neighborhood, so rare these days in bustling, bandbox Seattle. We walked through the rain past low-slung businesses selling things like maritime fittings and cheap Chinese food. Once upon a time, some man would've yelled something filthy at us as we walked. Or at least tried to talk to us. Once upon a time, leaving the house had a been a performance, an invitation, an engagement. No longer. We moved through the afternoon as clear and invisible as raindrops. Not that we noticed—we were in our mid-forties and this had been our condition for years.

"What year was that, when you moved to London?" I asked.

"It was 1984. God, I was so dumb when I was that age."

I immediately knew exactly what she meant.

She went on: "Like, when I reread my diaries and letters from that time, I was so stupid. It was just boys and drugs and drinking. I wish I could go back and tell myself to get over it. It was like I was blind to everything else in my life."

This sounded familiar to me. My own diaries were turning out to be appalling, a pageant of stupidity.

"I kinda miss being stupid," I said.

"Oh, you're still stupid," Vic said.

"Not *that* stupid."

Our sneakers were getting soaked through. We walked past the Safe N Sound swim school, into the wind. There was a smell of chlorine.

"At least we had feelings then," she said.

"Ugh, I was a slave to my feelings."

"At least we *had* them," she insisted.

"Do you think we've stopped? I feel like I can't get away from feelings. They sort of pin me down in bed."

"Oh, fuck, I don't know. I don't know what's wrong with me," she said. A single perfect tear leaked out, as if she were in a telenovela. She should have been holding a rose and wearing a gown. We kept walking, underneath the Fremont Bridge and then along the ship canal. The mineral-smelling lake water sloshed between cement walls. Geography: We had arrived at the middle of our lives, there on the rainy shore, and frankly it didn't look too hot.

October 30, 1989, age twenty-two

I want to fuck, I don't care who, I want to be fucked in the sink. I want a hand here, holding my world in place with a finger in my vagina. I want my breasts held and my face caressed. I want to feel that just holding still is enough, I want to be something without doing anything. I want to be essential and be fucked as such.

3

How to Have Sex with
Your Husband of Fifteen Years

First of all, I mean your husband you've been married to for fifteen years, not your fifteen-year-old husband. Don't be childish.

Nothing much is required in the way of supplies. Though supplies can be nice. When you use them with your husband of fifteen years, they are called marital aids. But you don't need them. Other things you don't need in order to have sex with your husband of fifteen years: compliments, nice underwear, dinner out, romance, very much time.

A thing you do require: a bed. Your husband of fifteen years might suggest the couch or the floor or the kitchen table. Demur. The family spaces are too, well, family-ish. They're marked by the product of sex: children.

Getting Started

Feel a surge of sexual yearning. This needn't be occasioned by your husband. It might be occasioned by thoughts of a stranger, or a dirty passage in a book, or a photograph of a glistening brown chicken in the Wednesday Food section of *The New York*

Times, or an errant breeze. Don't worry about where the yearning comes from, just be grateful you get to have it. The sexual yearning is an old friend, back to visit you from your youth. It disappeared for a while—for a long time—when you were a young mother. During that era your husband (then of fewer years) was the one who kept things moving along. Your husband's interest in sex was one of the things that made you interested in *him.* When you first met him, his shoe-gazing diffidence was both off-putting and alluring; you couldn't help but wonder what it would be like if he looked at you. If he touched you. When he firmly (dominantly?) took your hand for the first time, you felt an erotic shock and had this thought: "We are going to get married." Your husband wanted to do it all the time, when you were first married, and then all those years when the children were small. He wanted to do it inventively, sweetly, roughly, tenderly, filthily, chattily. Not you. Your body was used up by birth and by nursing, a tapped-out natural resource. Your husband carried the sex torch all those years. You had to talk yourself into it, and you had requirements. Date nights and intimacy. All that stuff. You don't have requirements now, just this tidal, ridiculous lust. I said it was an old friend, but it's more like old weather, a particular kind of rain that hasn't rained in a decade.

When the feeling comes, push or pull your husband onto the bed. Never mind that it's ten o'clock in the morning and you both have work to do. Never mind that you haven't brushed your teeth, or that you are wearing the tatty underpants you bought at Bartell Drugs seven years ago, though a look of wistful sadness will flit across your husband's face when you shuck your jeans and he sees the terrible panties that lie beneath. What does your husband of fifteen years think, that you're going to stop everything you are doing and rummage through your underwear drawer until you find something that is made of lace, something in one of those colors like burgundy or peach or teal that are mysteriously deemed sexy by manufacturers of fancy lingerie? Your husband of fifteen years is out of his mind if he thinks that is going to happen. And, trust me, he's not going to be deterred by your shabby undies—those drought years are fresh in his mind, and he never expected this mid-forties resurgence.

Your husband of fifteen years is a lot taller than you and hardly a delicate flower, so feel free to climb right on top of him and stick your tongue in his mouth. You're paying him back for all those years he did the hard work of being the aggressor. Do this for a while—put your tongue in his mouth, I mean. Kissing, like lust, has made a comeback. Kissing is having a moment. Kissing is back in black. Poke your tongue into the far reaches of his mouth. Let him do the same to you. When you were younger and you went around kissing pretty much everyone, you never gave a thought to germs. Now, kissing your own husband, think about germs. Think about how your bodies are dying and god only knows what's decaying inside your mouths. Feel obscurely aroused by this. Your husband flips you on your back and holds your hands over your head. Thoughts begin to fly away. There are many things that drive you nuts about your husband—his chronic untidiness, his occasional descents into grouchiness, and the way he kicks you (on purpose?) in his sleep—but there's also this. Him holding your hands over your head.

Ignore the refuse heap on the dresser: his receipts and change and thumb drives and sunglasses, all piled together. The heap is still there, but it's not piercing your consciousness with its usual sharp insistence. Begin to lose track of the house around you, with its order and its disorder and its demands and its chores. The spice drawer, with its loose drift of cinnamon. Begin to go underwater, into this secret Atlantean place where you lived when you were young and which you forgot about for all those years. Get up. Lock the bedroom door against the cat, against the rest of the world. The children are at school. Go back to bed.

Doing It

Kick the flowered quilt—bought that year you lived in Colorado, prized for its perfect weight—off the bed. Fit your body against your husband's. Smell your husband's smell. Unbutton his jeans. Reach into his boxer shorts and find his dick, like a joke every time. The hard-on is man's original slapstick. There's always something going on down there, even if it's nothing. Marriage is essentially plotless, but a dick has a plot. Something happens or doesn't happen, and suddenly you're in a story. Maybe this as much as anything else explains the resurgence of sex in your marriage. You yearn for plot as much as you yearn for dick, or you yearn for them together. Grab it, the way he likes, which he has been good and generous about telling you.

A theory about modern life: Everyone wants everyone else to dominate them. This is because we're so exhausted we want the other person to do all the work. Or maybe that's just you. Maybe you're projecting like crazy. But you do know that every once in a while your husband of fifteen years likes it if you do the work. So if you have even the tiniest bit of energy, push him down and scale him and lower yourself onto him. Hold his shoulders down firmly. If you're too fatigued to be the climber-onner, roll onto your back and draw your knees up toward your armpits and let him overwhelm you. Don't worry about your orgasm. Don't care about it. You've had a million orgasms in your life. Want only this. Want only total obliteration. In this way, too, you are returning to the girl you were—the girl who didn't care about orgasms but just wanted to fuck and fuck and fuck, without even knowing why. Those adult years of dutifully chasing clitoral orgasms—they seem alien in retrospect. Now you just want sensation, less definable than orgasm and weirdly more satisfying, more total.

Forget who you are. Forget who he is.

Don't think about the back of your left leg, where you recently spotted a single squiggling varicose vein, as fat and long as an udon noodle. Don't think about the wrinkly tags of skin on the backs of your elbows. Don't think about your eye bags. Don't think about those things, but do let their existence infuse you with wonder. There are those things, and there's also this. All at the same time. Stop thinking. Gasp for air. Make a cawing noise that you never make in any other circumstance.

Wrapping Up

Your husband of fifteen years will ask if you are done. He means, did you come. When you were younger, you would have said no, and he would have finished you, using his long beautiful dexterous finger. Instead, say yes. You are done. The obliteration-by-dick is, right now, this year, more obliterating than obliteration by means of actual orgasm. Try not to think about how this goes against every shoddily constructed feminist tenet you've ever held. You're done, like you said.

Now it's time for feedback. That was great, your husband will say. Or: That was wonderful. Or: That was different—as though he is a Midwestern lady at a potluck tasting a hot dish with too many spices. His ability to communicate about sex constantly amazes you, makes you shy, sometimes flat-out confuses you when you are stupid with what just happened. Say: Yes it was. Say: Wonderful, great, different. Mouth the words, even though you're still a mute passive animal, unable to render a verdict. The erasing of your critical function, of your ability to assess, of your *will,* was the point of the exercise in the first place. Know that your husband is himself, but he is also a stand-in for the rest of the world. Know that you want the men of the world to hold you down, to obliterate you, to take away the agency you spent so many years fighting for, cultivating, growing.

Your husband will jump up to get you a towel or a T-shirt and toss it to you. Mop yourself foolishly, absently. While your husband showers, stare out the window at the big cedar tree and think about mulching the garden.

Hear the mewling of the cat outside the door. Slide the bolt. Let the cat in.

June 21, 1983, age sixteen

All I write about is boys, boys, BOYS.

4.

A Kiss May Ruin a Human Life

I surveyed the diaries, twenty of them lined up in a row in chronological order. There were two large, plain, rectangular desks in my studio; I had arrayed the homely, worn journals—Mead notebooks, bound books, composition books, drawing pads—across one of these desks, a topographical timeline of twenty years of my life. If a person wanted to know about boys and yearning, this was definitely the place to look. I just had to sit down and read them, and maybe I'd finally understand this unease that had come over me. All would be revealed. Left to right, in chronological order: On the far left, my PEANUTS 1975 diary. I got it for Christmas when I was eight. I was so proud to have my own diary. I vowed I would write down everything that happened to me. I would write my feelings. I mean, if I happened to have any. Follow the domino path of shabby, well-thumbed volumes, and twenty diaries later, you come to the right-hand side of the desk: a black-and-red bound Chinese book whose last entry was—no shit—the night before my wedding. A girlhood ended. The writer in me couldn't help but be amazed at this narrative arc.

The diaries looked sort of totemic and weird lined up like this. Something casual, haphazard, unintended, almost spastic and certainly unconcerned with outcome or posterity had been organized and corralled, turned into a project. Though it is probably not accurate to say my diaries were unconcerned with posterity. I always believed, from age eight when I began my first diary, that I would have Readers.

The diaries' irresistible lure had to do with a larger problem, the world-terror that sometimes sent me to bed in the middle of the day, that howled at the door, no matter how cozy I was in the house with my funny children and my husband, who was always willing to chat with me, no matter the hour. My inability to get out of bed puzzled everyone. I thought maybe it was the flu. My doctor didn't know what was wrong with me. I remained convinced: the flu.

However. I had to leave the diaries and head off on my paperback tour. For the first few tour stops I brought along my children *and* my mother, which in retrospect should've tipped me off to just how crazy I was getting. The Northwest dates passed in a haze of cupcake shops and intergenerational bickering. My mom got chocolate-frosting stains on the upholstery of my Prius and I was elaborately patient about it.

Next up was a literary festival—ha!—at a big state university in a midsize city in the Southish Midwestish region. I don't know. You people in the South know where it begins and ends, but the rest of us aren't entirely sure. The first night, there was a reception and cocktail party, which in my current state of fake flu I dreaded. I checked into my hotel and called Victoria. I could picture her sitting in the tatty armchair in the corner of her painting studio. Over the chair's arm would be the chocolate-brown chenille throw she bought years ago at Crate & Barrel— she'd run into my mom there and the two of them picked it out together. Her booted feet would be resting, one over the other, on her footstool in that jaunty way of hers. I felt better just conjuring her image.

"I can't go out there," I said.

"You have to," she said. "You must. It's your job. I know you want to lie on your bed and watch TV, but you have to take care of your career whether you feel like it or not. It's like a pet. What are you going to wear?"

She talked me through which particular pair of black jeans, which particular clever black top from Anthropologie, which boots, and then she all but shoved me off the phone. "Call me before you go to bed, and you better have gone to the reception and you better have *talked to people!*"

I made my way to the hotel lobby, where, with a small group of friendly, dowdy writers, I looked over the list of the more-famous-than-me attending the festival. One name jumped out at me, a short-story writer from California who was very good and, for a short-story writer, very well known. "Oh! X is here!" I said to the group, and a woman snorted and mentioned something about his love of pretty young writers. "Isn't he married, though?" I asked, and she looked at me like I was a pathetic innocent. I felt an almost unconscious pinprick of interest: a famously immoral person! I wanted to know more. And also felt glad that I had blow-dried my hair. If I was going to meet an immoral person, I wanted to look my best. What I didn't quite acknowledge: I wanted him to try it on me. Whoever he was, whatever it was.

We all tromped over to the reception together: safety in numbers. The alleged party was held in a long light-filled room on the second floor of the university's architecturally ambitious humanities building. This being the South (I think), the room was prettily formal, with some uptight-looking antique furniture scattered around, a pinkish carpet, mirrors. The view was of the parking lot and, beyond, some rolling green hills that probably looked beautiful if you weren't from Washington State and didn't know better. I found myself in an eddy, on the edge of the room. I busied myself getting a plate of food. Never enough protein.

My two social modes these days seemed to be total fatigue or a wild, drunken abandon that ended with me in trouble. This had come out of nowhere, along with the sleepy despair of the last few months. Every once in a while I got drunk—in the passive voice, almost: It felt like it took hold of me, even though I was the fool doing the drinking. At a peaceful island birthday party one night when I'd gone totally bonkers, my friend Steve looked at me and said, "You know, you haven't blinked for several minutes."

Tonight, however, I was stuck in leaden-despair mode, as I often was at bookish parties. I could've been at home, surrounded by riches—Willie's eyes squinting with a joke he was about to unload, Lucy plucking away at her uke, Bruce dozing and pretending to read—but here I was. At least Victoria, at her art openings, got to hang out with patrons in their expensive black witchy clothes and their intelligent, uncomfortable shoes. Writers, on the other hand, get pilled sweaters and tote bags, because art is for rich people but books are for everyone. The grad students stood around in little clusters, observing the writers cackling, guzzling free wine. They were better-looking than us but we had careers. I could see how for a man this might look like a free-trade agreement. I felt like one of the students but tried to ignore the feeling.

A portly, tall, gray-haired person materialized in front of me. I was glad someone had appeared to talk to me; as Vic had so rightly surmised, I dreaded making an effort. The person wore an ill-fitting tweed blazer and a loosened silky tie. The two things didn't go together—his style was formal but somehow ramshackle or contingent. I found the contradiction touching. The show-offy tie, the not-up-to-it lumpy blazer. As a person feeling a bit vulnerable myself, I took this as a kind of sign or maybe just a reminder that other people were not perfectly comfortable or at ease either.

He was peering cheekily at the name tag on my chest: "Claire Dederer," he read. He rhymed it with Federer, which most people do. Roger Federer is responsible for much mispronouncing of my name. "You reviewed me!" he exclaimed. It was the famous (and famously libidinous, a fact that had positively *lodged* in my brain) Californian short-story writer, and he was peering at me with great interest, like I was an objet in a curio shop. In fact, he was openly assessing me from head to toe. He looked as if he wanted to give me a poke, to see if I was as high-quality as I appeared. I liked it. His fame and his cheekiness and his vulnerable sports coat all made me feel suddenly a little . . . high.

"I did?" I asked. "Did I think you were any good?" I reviewed a lot, right after my first child was born, sometimes several books a month, and I was something of a—how to say this?—hatchet man.

"Yes, it was a very nice review," he said. "You loved it. You were probably too generous, if anything." I couldn't tell if he was teasing. Or implying I was stupid.

"Asparagus!" he said, looking at my plate. "They shouldn't have!"

"There's a buffet. Do you want to get yourself some food?" I asked, mom-ishly.

"That's okay, I'll just have yours," he said, and took a spear off my plate and sword-swallowed it with extravagant silliness. He began to quiz me: "Where are you from? . . . An island near Seattle?! . . . Two kids?!" Every answer I gave seemed to fill him with delight—a delight so vividly expressed that I thought it must be ironic. I couldn't quite tell. It was a year or two before I realized how drunk he'd been that night. He was doing all the dumb classic flirt things, touching my arm, teasing me about the way I was inhaling my food, but he overlaid it with a kind of self-mocking irony. "Oh may I?" he asked with elaborate courtesy, before drinking my drink. He seemed to be somehow sending up the awkwardness of the situation; even though he was famous, one of the rulers of the room, and even though he was obeying the conventions of the party—chatting, sipping—there was something about him that was simultaneously acknowledging its inherent awkwardness and subverting it. Something about him, like me, didn't quite fit. Maybe, probably, everyone in the room felt the same way, but he, with his ridiculously overt flirting and his assertive interestedness, made it fun.

"I've got to hit the can," he said. He paused for a moment, and gave me a look that was, if possible, even more intent than the way he'd been looking at me before. I felt myself grow hot, and after he walked away, looked in one of the cheesy rococo mirrors. I was very pink. Embarrassingly pink. Well, he was gone now. I drifted off to talk to the grad students, who were clustered around a famous poet (like *that's* a thing). With the disappearance of the story writer, the scene seemed grimmer and duller than ever. I would get through the rest of the evening somehow, and then go back to the hotel and watch a movie.

After a few minutes, the story writer found me, which unto itself was thrilling. He gripped my biceps, probably harder than he needed to, and pulled me away from the group. Some little engine in me started up. Being looked at, being grabbed, being pulled—it felt good. I subconsciously tamped down the feeling. He dragged me through the room and onto an empty corner of the balcony. The hills were looking very green; I guess I could see how someone might write a country song about them or whatever.

"Now!" he said importantly, and began to drill me about my writing. Why had I quit reviewing, what was my book about? For of course a man like him, a man of standards, the kind of man who would wear a tie to a wine-'n'-cheese thing—a man like that would not have read a *yoga memoir*. Desperately I tried to turn the questions back on him, but he wouldn't let me, he just kept getting me glasses of wine and asking me things. Not that that's any excuse. Finally we started comparing notes on people we knew in common.

"Oh, her book was terrible!" I said of a mutual acquaintance.

"You should've seen it before I edited it for her," said he, and I could tell by his smile that he'd slept with her. He was as a pane of glass to me. Maybe he was like that with everyone, or maybe it was just because I was so immediately, so entirely *interested* in him.

I confess his sinning was what interested me. He was so ridiculously, overtly on the make, it sort of took me aback and even impressed me. Here I was, being so good, trying to keep my shit together, trying to be better than the craptastic girl I'd been, and he was just running around being bad. I didn't know anyone bad (or thought I didn't—more on that later). I wanted to keep watching him in action. Maybe I would like to, um, receive some action.

When he told me he would drive me in his rental car to the next event, a reading, I said yes. He hadn't asked, anyway. He had told.

Once in his car, I sat back and put my booted feet up on the dashboard: "Can I put my feet up?"

"Do whatever you like," he said, with a sideways look. It was so long since I'd been seen just like that. My husband told me I was pretty every day, practically, but this was a pure objectification—he was object-ing me. We drove through the night, which was warm and funny-smelling, close, like being trapped in a French kiss.

I mentioned how much I'd liked the famous poet's über-preppy getup. "Everything was so rumpled. Even his collar was rumpled. It was weirdly sexy," I said, a piece of gentle provoca-tion. The story writer rumpled his own collar with a significant look. I was suddenly appalled—I was *flirting*—and gazed at my feet.

How quickly it became real country here; the dark spaces between streetlights grew longer and longer. I leaned my head back, a passenger. I asked him idly if he knew the Iggy Pop song "The Passenger," one of my very favorites. "I am the pas-senger / and I ride and I ride," it goes. The passivity of riding and never driving. A fantasy of mine. At home, I always insisted on driving; after all, I knew the way. But I realized all of a sud-den that I loved this. I loved being the passenger. I loved having the story writer drive me bossily through the night. I ignored the fact that at home I was so bossy that I wouldn't even let my husband drive. I wouldn't let him let me be the passenger. I couldn't do that at home for some reason. Here among the (Southern?) green hills, I loved giving up control, I loved the stars in the countryish darkness.

"What?" replied the writer. "No. Iggy Pop? He's pretty bad, right?"

Sigh. These were my people now that I was a writer, people who didn't understand anything. I mean, they understood per-fectly the thing I cared most about—books—but basically were moron-level elsewhere. "Never mind."

"We're going for a drink," he said, and pulled into the park-ing lot of a Mexican restaurant. Where *was* I?

"Won't we be late for the reading?" I asked. I was concerned in some obscure way about getting in trouble, but also I didn't want my good name linked to his bad name. It was like I knew that my devil self would be exposed just by proximity to him. This intuition was correct, as it happened.

As we got going on our drinks, he said, "Y'know, I've thought several times about just planting one on you."

Oh! I would really, really like that, I didn't say. I couldn't think of anything nicer than having this person plant one on me at that exact moment. I felt it in my undies, as one does, but somewhere else too. Maybe my imagination? That faculty was so exercised, so *awake*, it felt like a flesh thing, an organ, all of a sudden, as I pictured what might happen: his mouth on mine, all that newness and strangeness. I maybe fell into a gape-mouthed reverie? And shook myself out of it. Jesus, I was getting played. It'd been awhile, and my defenses were for shit. I felt wobbly. Even so, I laughed and said, "I've never done that. I'm pretty married."

He gave me a disbelieving look. "You've never kissed any-one besides your husband in—how long? How many years have you been married?"

"Fifteen years. But we were together for a year before that and I never cheated on him." Fact. "So sixteen years since I've kissed someone else."

"Just . . . Wow." We gazed at each other over the crevasse that lay between our world views: his flagrancy, my virtuousness. My virtuousness, which on some level I knew was a veneer or an overlay.

"Well, what's the worst thing you *have* done?" he asked, set-tling left ankle onto right knee, leaning forward, really inter-ested.

"This," I said. But I smiled at him. Love me, said my smile.

The next day, another party; this time a dull patrons' dinner at a country club. I chatted glumly with the punters, doing my duty. I was seated next to the grande dame of the festival, a kind of oracular lit-fest lizard in love with her own candor. "Your author photo isn't doing you any favors, my dear," she said. As I listened to her wheeze on with the self-confidence of the person who is footing the bill, I watched the short-story writer, I hoped covertly. But I kept catching his eye. He circulated elegantly, creating little puddles of intimacy at every stop. He hunched toward whomever he was talking to, semaphoring interest. I found this annoying. I wanted his interest. I wanted him to semaphore things to *me*. His strange combination of comfort and discomfort, his clear need to be loved, his compulsive flirting—I wanted it all for myself. It was as if he'd taken all my faults and recooked the ingredients into something delicious and irresistible. Probably I wanted his fame too. Probably.

Finally we all trooped off to yet another party, where I slipped into my manic mode. I drank and drank, rocketing around the party like a pinball. My dysphoric apprehension at the previous night's reception had turned into the kind of slightly hostile madcappery that wants to lay to waste everything it meets.

I pushed every conversation to its edge, starting fights and making inappropriate jokes. I stopped blinking. In fact, I departed my body altogether, and somehow other people knew it, knew there was an empty body floating around that they could put to use. I was forty-five. You wouldn't think people would want to occupy my vacated body—who wants to take up with a body that's half a century old? My body was the heaviest it had ever been (without another human growing inside it), my hair was frizzy, and my skin was as the arctic tundra. But apparently a vacated body, and the attendant frisson it creates, is just that alluring. Someone put his hand down my shirt. Someone else gave me his room number. Etc. "Everyone needs a place. It shouldn't be inside of someone else," writes Richard Siken in the poem "Detail of the Woods." But I left the door wide open— come on in.

Finally some kind soul gently told me she'd take me back to my hotel. As I stumbled out the door, the Californian story writer, who'd been in the back of my mind all along, grabbed my hand and pulled me—again with the pulling!—up the street away from the party. Heart-leafed catalpas spread over the side-walk. I was revisited by that feeling that we had all the same faults; we were just *expressing* them to different degrees. We swung our knitted fists like brother and sister, up the block, in the dark, until I felt my arm yanked hard, and his hand on the back of my head, the way you might steady an infant, and I was kissed. It wasn't even a kiss, it was a penetration, all the way to the back molars. When he said he wanted to plant one on me, he really meant he wanted to plant one *in* me.

The streetlamp spangled in the catalpas and I found myself falling through a wormhole into a hallucination. I saw the future. It was as if I were one of those characters in a sci-fi movie, fall-ing through kaleidoscopic swirling colors into the future, time-traveling from the present into the *what was going to happen for sure:* This kiss would make me guilty and excited and full of sharp pain for the lost purity of my marriage. This would go on for months or for god knew how long. I would be tor-mented by it, and this person, this kisser, would not under-stand my torment. I would care, and he would not. Why should he? Just a kiss. All in a day's work for someone of his nature. This, it seemed, was being old and being kissed: You knew too much.

All of this occurred, in proper sci-fi fashion, within a split second, before the story writer had even really released me from his impulsive grip. And so, as we stepped back from each other, I scowled at him, who had become my enemy in the hallucina-tory future.

"This is not nothing," I hissed. And then—I fear it is true—I stamped my foot. I was furious, because suddenly what had been a perfectly faithful marriage was sundered; my track record was soiled; worst of all, my bulwark against the bad girl

I'd been now bore a fatal chink. Others might see it as just a kiss, but I felt a blow, a premonition.

"Let's go back," he said brusquely. "They'll be missing us." And so I began to live out the strange, lonely terms of my hallucination.

I called Vic from my hotel room. Then I called Bruce. I was trying to find my people in the dark. They were cross and muzzy with sleep. I'd woken them up. Call me back tomorrow, they said. I was on my own, and tossed and turned through the night. What I remembered was the driving, and the pulling, and the incursion. I didn't want to do it. He made me. There was something wonderful in him making me. Was that what I really wanted? To be made to do it? It was an upsetting thought.

In the morning there was a funny e-mail from him. He'd looked up an article I'd written about Raymond Carver. He said he thought I was cool. I groaned, as if in pain. He knew how to get under my skin: looking me up, calling me cool. He was reading me as easily as I'd read him. Or maybe anybody and everybody would like these things; maybe I just wanted to be seen, to be read, to be pulled, to be kissed by someone new. Maybe the short-story writer was simply *who was there;* maybe anybody would've done.

The next morning I got on a plane and headed to another city whose geography was imperfectly understood by me: Tulsa, Oklahoma. I passed through Dallas, where I watched a gray storm move around outside the airport windows. I had thought Texas was sunny, but this whole gigantic corner of our nation seemed to be on eternal tornado watch. Flatness is not as safe as it seems. In Tulsa they put me in a little hotel in a sketchy part of town. Hard by the freeway, plastic bags blowing around the street, pit bulls behind insufficient-looking chain-link fencing. My host was a young man who ran a literary series. He was a lovely guy, single-handedly bringing all kinds of authors to Tulsa, and what's more, getting Tulsans to come see the authors. You can get authors to go anywhere, to the ends of the earth, to Tulsa even; it's getting their audience to leave the house that's diffi-cult. More important, he was fun. He wanted to go out for meals and yak. He wanted to drive me around Tulsa and show me shit. He wanted to gossip about famous writers he'd lured to town. He spoke boastfully of the "Tulsa Sound." As a dedicated provin-cial I appreciated his boosterism.

We were eating burritos and gossiping when he looked at me sadly. "I almost didn't even read your book," he said, mean-ing my yoga memoir.

I nodded, immediately understanding. For all his virtues, he was, after all, a guy.

He went on. "When it came in the mail, I opened the pack-age and I was like, *lady book.*" He pantomimed chucking my book over his shoulder into some imaginary pile of unreadable crap.

Well, what did I expect? I wrote a book about being a housewife and a mom. As if that weren't enough, my book was a mother/daughter memoir. As if that weren't enough, it dealt with the theme of women's lib. And then I wrapped the whole thing up in yoga, like a scallop wrapped in bacon.

Sometimes I regretted having written such a very female book. After all, I didn't feel like a lady. I felt more like a seventeen-year-old boy: horny, sleepy, confused. In fact, I rather wished I were a boy, or a man. And why not? The good things come to boys. Male authors don't have to explain why their themes—war, or baseball, or anal sex if you're James Salter—are important. When female organizers of literary series get a book on a boy topic, they don't throw it over their shoulder with a disparaging *guy book*. Or if they do, they certainly don't mention it to the author later over burritos.

I said something soothing and understanding—I'm a lady, after all, and of course I wanted him to like me—and we drank another beer. I went back to my room and lay on my bed, watching *New Girl* episodes on my iPad. Lady, lady, lady. I turned off my iPad and shut my eyes. The story writer was so present it was almost as though he were sitting on top of me, like a very literate, slightly rumpled incubus. He wouldn't get off either. All the darkness, all the dirty feelings I'd been having, all the longing, all the teen passion, all the loneliness now had somewhere to live: inside that dumb disruption of a kiss. And I didn't even have to be responsible for it. I was a passenger.

September 2, 1983, age sixteen

I find my thoughts, no not my thoughts so much as my dreams, are becoming disturbingly permeated by John. I thought I wasn't going to do this anymore, it's so stupid.

5

Pomegranates

Bruce got invited on a *National Geographic* expedition—he was asked to document James Cameron's dive to the bottom of the Mariana Trench. He would be gone a month, maybe longer. (In the event, it took three; he went from Sydney, to Guam, to Yap, to an unnamed atoll.) I was unsure how I'd fare on my own: There was a bouquet of deadlines, and kid duty, and me with my diminished capacity. But what kind of asshole would tell her adventure-writer husband he can't go on a *National Geographic* expedition to explore a deep-sea trench? With one of the world's leading egomaniacs? Especially when the trip would fund our family for a year? Especially *especially* when my only reason to keep him home would sound something like this: "Um, I'm kind of . . . sad? And I seem to have the flu, although the doctor says it's definitely not. The flu."

The night before he left, he was packing his expeditiony clothes—the kind of sink-washable shirts and pants with bits you can roll up or zip off or snap back; every item must convert into some other item. I told him I might leave the kids with my mom for a weekend and take a break with Vic, maybe in L.A. As he loaded a pair of cargo pants with zip-off legs into his dry sack he said, "You know, on one of these jaunts you take, you're going to meet someone. Some other writer, someone older than you. Something is going to happen. Just be careful." I blushed and said surely not. He gave me a look and went back to packing, and then the next day he was gone, on a flight to Sydney.

I was not the picture of efficiency in Bruce's absence. He was, after all, the organizing principle of my life. He brought me coffee in bed each morning and instilled in me a certain sense of shame if I lingered there too long. He chatted with me about work and bickered with me about the dishes. Because he was a naturally anxious type, his worry about getting enough done each day kept me on track. Though I'd been self-employed for many years, I'd never had to develop self-discipline—I just slipstreamed on Bruce's. Without him there, things went pretty much to pot. I left the keys in the front door overnight—outside. I lay in bed all day and read Spalding Gray's journals rather than doing my chores or my work. I lost my wallet. I neglected to pay the bills. I forgot to pick the children up from activities. I left the oven on.

It was the winter of my forty-fifth year. Winter meant rain and darkness and children with persistent coughs. The house resounded with painful barking. There was a brackish pong in the air. However, one good thing came with winter: pomegranates. Every October, I'd start asking the solemn-faced guy in the Town & Country produce department if they'd come yet. All summer long they were gone, just gone, and then they appeared as if by some gorgeous magic, no biggie, the most beautiful food in the world. I suppose I could've done something about it, made myself knowledgeable, learned all about them, maybe written a pithy, witty little article about them, but I preferred the magic. Here they were, until they weren't. The first ones were sour and expensive: $5.99 for a single pom with pale pink nothing-tasting seeds. But I bought them anyway, just for the weight of it in my hand and the good, all-in moment of slicing its top off and going to work on it. I ate one a day, dosing myself with seeds.

I couldn't keep my head together. The incubus/kisser came most nights and perched on me. I never got used to him, and he kept being an incubus. I didn't want to think of him as a cheesy old incubus. I wanted to think of him as at least a more literary monster and not one that had the same name as a terrible rock band. But incubus is what he was. He excited and upset me, and I woke unrefreshed, with grainy, empty eyes, and went through my day simultaneously aroused and exhausted. I told Vic, "People shouldn't kiss housewives who haven't kissed anyone besides their husband in more than fifteen years. It fucks a housewife up!"

Never mind my parenting; my work was falling apart. I made a fairly major error in a story, and a correction had to be printed, and the story surrounding the error wasn't any good anyway. I seemed to have forgotten how to write. There was something between me and the work; my relationship to it was curiously muffled. I was a woman in a bear suit, trying to type with paws instead of hands.

I was able to get out of bed to drive people to school, to cook dinner, to see Victoria. We continued to go on our long gray walks. I came into the city and we flung ourselves around the edge of the lake. We saw other women our age doing the same thing: walking, intent, ceaselessly talking, trying to solve their seemingly perfectly okay lives. Vic's face crumpled like a napkin and she was crying again. Then we saw a crow fall over—what? that happens?—and we started cracking up again. The whole situation reminded me of these beautiful lines about Death Valley from the novelist Nancy Lemann: "It's so godforsaken . . . that you are curiously elated. It may be called Death Valley, but the minute you get there you are subsumed by a vast and incongruous gaiety." If you substitute "middle age" for "Death Valley," this perfectly describes our feelings.

We walked through the rain, which was so incessant that it's like saying we walked through the air. We'd both had barren mornings. I couldn't write. She couldn't seem to make anything.

"It's a scrim," I said.

"What do you mean, a scrim?"

"It's like a scrim between me and anything I try to write. No matter what I'm working on. I'm not ever quite . . . touching it. There's an obstacle."

"A scrim."

"Yes."

She quoted from the Isaac Mizrahi documentary *Unzipped:* "I scrim, you scrim, we all scrim for the scrim!"

"Ha ha. It's not funny. The scrim is ruining my life."

She walked in silence for a bit, and then said, "I think I have one too."

We walked on, thinking scrim thoughts, with chapped lips. Tundra everywhere.

In Seattle I was haunted by ghosts on every corner—ghosts of kisses. Memories popped up everywhere I turned. It was a relief to take the ferry home, from my old Gomorrah to the safety of my island. When I picked up Lucy that afternoon, she was quiet. We drove along under the tossing Douglas firs, whose crenellated boughs somehow recalled oyster shells. Her friend and carpool-mate Julia chattered about social plans for the weekend; Lucy grew, if possible, quieter. She was now in eighth grade, which as it happens is not the easiest year for most humans. I wanted to help, but who knows if people that age can actually even be helped. People in eighth grade, like toddlers, are in an ongoing crisis of becoming. Lucy seemed to need me physically, as she had when she was little. It was as if she, a balloon trying to lift into glorious, terrifying flight, wanted to tether herself to this planet with my body. We lay on the couch that night, on-demanding *Project Runway,* our legs in a tangle.

At the grocery store the previous day I had seen a toddler throwing a fit and I thought, God, it's so hard being little. All that *want* and you're not sure how to *get.* Then I thought: This is the perfect description of eighth grade. I'm surprised all eighth-graders don't just lie down on the grocery-store floor and drum their heels against the linoleum and weep out of sheer frustration. And then I thought: This is the perfect description of middle age. Lucy and I were both in a state of ongoing crisis; we were holding each other down, keeping each other from floating away; all we needed was a two-year-old to hang out with to complete our triumvirate.

So that was one thing I could do, one thing that in the midst of my new uselessness I was still capable of: I could be present for Lucy's existential crisis. Though who knows if she felt like I was good company or any company at all—I certainly had felt perfectly alone in my own eighth-grade existential crisis. (Compare my diary from that year: "There's no reason I should be lonely.") Aside from snuggling Lucy through the apocalypse, I felt pretty no-account.

Each day I would rise, make breakfasts and lunches, get children to school, and then I'd come home and open whatever document I was supposed to be working on, and then I'd just clamber hopelessly back in bed. Our bank account was dwindling due to my lack of ability to complete any work. The kisser would e-mail me sometimes and I didn't know which was worse: hearing from him or not. His stand-in, the incubus, hung around, looking elegant and scary in the purple armchair in the bedroom, one leg slung over the other. And I lay there and let him, or anyway the feelings he engendered, invade my whole life.

Pomegranates

. . .

It was just e-mails turning up every once in a while. What was new with his family, his work, his friends. Certainly not love letters; just letters. But they baked into me a yearning of such intensity that I was stupid and hot with it. My very in-box took on a different and altogether emotional aspect; it seemed illuminated or cast in gloom depending on whether or not it housed a letter from my be-liked. I thought about him when I woke up in the morning; but what was I thinking about? I had known him for only a day or two; aside from that, he was not even words on a page. He was that modern phenomenon, marks on a screen.

The yearning felt familiar to me; I recognized it dimly, like a face in an airport. The intense self-regard, the construction of the self in relation to the other, the vain, insecure display— of course I knew it all too well. This was what it had been like to be young. This was what I had spent my time doing for years and years: yearning for the other (even when I was in his arms), manipulating the other, charming the other, worrying what the other thought of me. This was obsession. And like all such obsessions, it had more to do with me than it did with its object. I noticed that I read my own e-mails at least as carefully as I read his. I didn't wonder about him and his home life very much; I did wonder what he thought about me as he sat around in his office. I couldn't picture him very well, but I looked in the mirror more often. Obsession: not exactly the same thing as love, which is more interested in its object. I was preening for a male higher up on the food chain. It was not a case of "I love you," but a case of "Love me."

Being seen, being objectified, even if in some obscure way I was just doing it to myself: It felt so good as I slid into invisibility. I craved it again, though for so long I'd been content with Bruce's gaze. After all, I was seen in toto in my house. My husband did nothing but see me from his wide-set blue eyes. He looked at me every day like he couldn't believe he got to be married to me. But somehow his regard had become less important, or unhelpful. I'd forgotten how to value it. I told myself his lustful regard for me was just another way I was utile—he was constantly delighted by the idea that there was a woman in his very own home whom he could fuck. I felt so low, I couldn't help but wonder: Would anyone have done?

I considered myself in the mirror and I didn't know what I was looking at. In fact, I was delusional, and the delusion was ongoing and insidious. For instance: I had gained some weight. Fifteen pounds. Here's a piece of advice. Don't gain fifteen pounds once you are past, say, forty-two. Don't gain one pound. It is a full-time job to remove it. The only way to do it is to Not Eat. Fuck a healthy diet and exercise. You have to stop eating. And then you're mean to your kids and then you want to die. So just don't gain the weight. Anyway, delusion: When I gained my fifteen pounds, I looked in the full-length mirror that fate has placed on the closet door in our bedroom. My legs and arms looked much the same as ever, but when I turned sideways, I saw what appeared to my disbelieving eyes to be a proud gut arching away from my body. The gut started just below my breasts and it curved outward from there to just above my undies, where it sort of slumped into a heap. It was like having a flesh-covered talus attached to the front of my body. Here's the delusion part. I looked at my new stomach and literally had this thought: "This is what I'd look like if I were fat." Same thing goes for all the other physical indignities of aging: the wattles, the gray hair, the wrinkles. I looked at them and thought, "This is what I'd look like if I were old."

I had been gazed at by men for so long, had craved it, hated it, recoiled from it, loved it. Then it went away. Now in this strange, utterly safe, long-distance way, I was being regarded by a stranger again. I became dependent on it, perhaps because I was, like Lucy, unsure of myself and of whom and what I was. The man regarding me was putting me back together again, as men had done so many times before.

Every day I ate a pomegranate. I learned a good method for opening them from a YouTube video: cut off the top, slice along the fruit walls, pull apart. Martha Stewart has a no-fail method for shaking all the seeds loose at once, but the picking at the fruit was the most important part for me. I loved pulling each little seed from the white flesh. I never got over the satisfied feeling that came when the glowing little thing came free. And it was such a neurotic-*looking* activity. I liked the way it externalized my despair. Each night, after the children were in bed, I drank a water glass full of bourbon, and this too pleased me. These were my acts of desperation: lying in bed, drinking lonely bourbon, picking at my seedy fruit.

Vic was falling apart more glamorously over in the city, with things like cigarettes and art openings. I had isolated myself from that, in my house in the country, where I had thought I would be safe. But I wasn't safe, just isolated. I believed my cohort, my fellowship, the formerly weird, the troubled, the angsty, the fucked-up was nowhere to be seen here on my island. People on my island were life's winners. Most had cruised through college and on to grad school, galleons in full sail. Or so I told myself— that old adolescent fallacy: Everyone else is fine.

I went on eating my poms and feeling misunderstood by the world. Because pomegranates stain so much, I had a special, spectacularly depressing hoodie I wore when I ate them. It was a blah gray marked all over with bloody pom spots.

.   .   .

Vic gently suggested that I see a shrink. I hit up an old Jungian on my island named Gerald. Gerald practiced in a pole barn and delivered his thoughts from a knockoff Eames lounge chair, which somehow seemed even more shrinky than an authentic Eames lounge chair. His person was classically shrink-like too: He had fabulous eyebrows like fronds, or antennae designed to pick up extra psychodata about his client. His hair looked like a cloud that had accidentally landed on his head, and his clothes looked like they'd been put on in the dark. His mind was on higher things. Even better: His mind was on me.

One day I showed up in my pomegranate sweatshirt. As I settled into the cushy patient chair, I laughingly explained the stains to him. I was always quite shameless about trying to entertain Gerald and make him love me. When he heard about the pomegranate stains, he basically freaked the fuck out. At least I think that is the technical term for it. "WHAT? You've been eating POMEGRANATES?" he asked.

"I ate a pomegranate before I came here. I eat one every day."

He left a long, meaningful pause. "You are aware, aren't you, that you're living out the Persephone myth."

"I don't think so—she was a maiden, and she was abducted."

"You aren't a maiden? You might be a mother, but you're remarkably immature in the way you worry about what other people think of you, and the way you cling to security." Yes, my shrink just told me I was immature.

He went on: "You're not alone. A lot of people don't give up their younger selves until they're in their mid-forties."

I figured a little more: "So I was taken by Hades"—that meant the kisser—"and now I'm where? In hell?"

"You tell me. It would seem that way."

"But I was already in hell before I met that fucking e-mailer. I was already depressed."

"Well, I'm not saying you followed a script. These things don't work like that." More silence, more beneficent gazing from under his brows. Gee, he was a nice man. Just palpably *nice.* "What often gets forgotten in the Persephone story is the importance of Demeter. Persephone is creating a break from her mother. Another way of looking at it: By getting herself abducted, she creates a break from what's expected of her as a woman—a break from the motherhood that is her destiny. Demeter is safety, expectation, motherhood. Persephone yearns to be free of all that. So she goes and gets herself abducted."

Fucking Gerald.

After three months, Bruce finally came home from the trench. In fact we met him halfway, the kids and I—we hooked up with him at the Honolulu airport. I planned my outfit days in advance. Thought about how to make my hair look right when I got off the plane. Made sure the children were neat and clean. He appeared in the Hawaiian Airlines concourse, ruddy and tall and grinning, and I attached myself to him, patting his back and sides, checking him for reality. Yup. After he'd snuggled the children, I led him to the funny smoking garden in the center of the Honolulu airport, a place of trimmed misshapen grass patches and low salmon-colored walls—someone's bright 1960s idea. We walked around and around the garden, getting used to each other. Like all formal gardens—even cheesy ones like this—it was as though one was walking through a map or a schema of a small world. I clung to Bruce's arm. Save me, I thought. That night we had sex in the hotel room adjacent to our children's, whispering to each other what we wanted to do, what we were doing. Remaking our little world through language. When we were done, I lay on top of him. STAY. PUT. I didn't let him out of my sight for days.

But once we were back at home, nothing had really changed, except now I was morbidly self-aware about my pomegranate consumption. The moment I sliced off the top of the pom, a moment that used to be one of uncomplicated joy, now felt a bit fraught. Unless I happened to be the receiver of unsolicited hugs from my children, the pom was the brightest spot of my day. Except for the bourbon. My world had become very small, in the way of addicts. This island: I had chosen smallness, safety. What's safer than an island? During this period, the children sometimes discussed the coming zombie apocalypse, and they and their friends agreed it was good that we lived on an island. An island is safe and contained and one's choices are necessarily limited by living within its parameters. Like, um, what's that other thing? Oh, marriage. I chose this constraint, the constraint of marriage. I had chosen it in part because I was afraid of what would happen in the absence of constraints. I was pretty sure such a life, for me, would lead to chaos. Without the order of family life, without the specific tender witness and deliberateness and sweetness of Bruce himself, I would spin into who knows what outer darkness. And his own nature, as a person who reflexively chooses constraint and opts for refusal, would turn him into a fatal isolato. Or so I thought. And yet—hadn't he slipped the constraint? No biggie—only as far as, you know, *Yap*. It didn't occur to me that he might be chafing a little too.

There can be a lot of goodness in constraint. It's like Anne Fadiman wrote about the sonnet: It might look small, but you could fit the whole world in there if you shoved hard enough. Or look at the pomegranate, for heaven's sake, a finite tiny globe but containing such complexity and weirdness and even glory. Look at this little round fruit, a world you can heft in one hand, with its almost creepy teeming interior life.

November 13, 1982, age fifteen

There is no reason I should be lonely.

6.

The, You Know,
Encroaching Darkness

The lure of bed; the lure of being asleep. The spring I was forty-five it called to me more and more. I wanted to be unconscious; short of that I wanted *to not think*. There were so many things that I couldn't bear to think about; better and easier to pull the covers over my head. I went to dinner with my friend Emily who said, apropos of I can't remember what, "I have a whole list of shit I refuse to think about." I hadn't realized other people were refusing to think about stuff too, hadn't realized other people had these no-go areas. But of course, I realized, staring at Emily, adult life must be full of these blacked-out areas. This is why we go to bed depressed, or fantasize about affairs, or drink too much wine. I went home and asked the oracle: Facebook. What don't you want to think about? I asked, feeling embarrassed. Maybe, after all, Emily and I were the only ones with such a list. But no, the grown-ups were happy, even excited, to provide the lists of stuff they don't want to think about, and it turned out to be mostly . . . drains. Here's the list:

My dripping bathroom faucet.
Slow death.

The, You Know, Encroaching Darkness

My children talking about me the way I have talked
    about my parents.

I may not be precisely current on my federal taxes.

I have a phobia about water pipes. I try not to think
    about them, but they're at the back of my mind
    most of the day.

Ways I could've been kinder to my now-dead husband.

I still don't understand how insurance works.

Global consolidation of power and decay of empathy.

Alzheimer's.

Species extinction.

What my boobs will look like in 2032.

One day our bathroom floor will collapse since very
    often when someone showers, enough water
    escapes the curtain so that there's a little puddle in
    the corner between the tub and sink that finds its
    way through the tile and presumably dampens and
    molds and weakens the floorboards before it drip
    drip drips onto the washing machine below.

Rats.

Health insurance.

Earthquake.

My aging parents.

The, you know, encroaching darkness.

My car's engine light.

My kids leaving.

Flossing.

Debt.

How I have scarred my kids.

The dirt in cracks I can't get to.

Plumbing issues I can't fix myself.

Money. I don't even like to look at my account activity.

Mean ways I treated people when I was young and
    stupid.

Breast cancer.

Cruelty to children.

Who will keep the house clean when I am dead.

Bedbugs.

Norovirus.

Losing control of mind and body as I age.

Female genital mutilation.

Super bugs.

Old pipes.

All the times I know I could have been a better
    father—those moments when I knew better but
    didn't do better.

The planet's lack of potable water.

My parents fixing to die just when I started to like
    them.

The years wasted on the wrong projects, places, self-
    conceptions.

What would happen if our landlord raised our rent to
    market value?

Various occasions upon which I have humiliated
    myself.

The earth dying.

Face sag.

Child porn.

Varicose veins.

Dying alone, i.e., the fate of every single human.

April 12, 1980, age thirteen

Went to see a double feature of movies about the Who with Steph last night. Her family lives in the fast lane. Her stepdad Joe came home to the boat, drunk, made a phone call, tried to kiss me, and left.

7

Dear Roman Polanski

Dear Roman Polanski,

You will never read this. Seriously. Why would you read the words of a crabby mother of two, a housewife who lives on a rural(ish) island near Seattle? Who cares what I think? Not you, I am sure. On the other hand, Roman Polanski, as I grow older I think about you more and more often. In fact, sometimes I find I can't stop thinking about you. Is it because I have a thirteen-year-old daughter, the age Samantha Gailey was when you raped her? That seems kind of, I dunno, obvious. And yet that's when you appeared in my mind, like the squirrel who once moved into the crawl space above my kitchen. I sat down to write, at my spacious desk in my office, a plate of cookies at my elbow, and you appeared. And now, like someone practicing automatic writing, I find myself writing you a letter.

Yours is a name that's been in my head ever since I can remember. First and foremost as a kind of bogeyman. I was born in 1967; you released *Rosemary's Baby* in 1968; Charles Manson murdered your pregnant wife Sharon Tate in 1969. So from the time I was conscious you were associated with horror, both imagined and real. Even your name was devilish (same first name as the Satan-worshipping neighbor in *Rosemary's Baby*, in fact). Roman: suggestive of things imperially perverted, unwholesome, *European*. Polanski: sounds like Polack, which in the 1970s connoted a joke. Altogether the very definition of *not okay*. I knew the name because of *Helter Skelter*, Vincent Bugliosi's 1974 account of the Manson murders, a volume that was everywhere in my 1970s. Grown-ups seemed to be issued this book along with their driver's licenses. Everyone read it. As a kid, I couldn't avoid it, even if it upset me to look at the cover; even if, whenever I peeked inside at the photos, I got a terrible stomachache. There it was, everywhere, a reminder that things we didn't understand were happening all around us. Reminding us of dirtiness out there, sullying even the pristine white Beatles, after whose song Manson named his bloody revolution. Out There was dangerous. I already had some idea of how bad it could get. When I was a kid—how to frame this, efficiently, within the confines of a letter? after all, even an imaginary letter must have confines—my favorite uncle, beautiful young funny Uncle Tim, was shot to death by his boyfriend. And then, the same year, my mother's lover's brother—a kind of uncle, but wasn't everyone a kind of uncle then?—disappeared while making a drug buy in the mountains of Mexico. Seventies deaths. Freedom deaths. So Out There wasn't just a threat. It had come In Here already. But *Helter Skelter*—well, that was a reminder it could always get worse, was always getting worse.

And then of course there was the other thing. The rape—or was it? You went to trial just as I was becoming sentient at the age of ten. You had done something terrible. I wasn't sure what. Back then sex itself seemed terrible, and any deviation from the norm horrifying. I remember the grade school buzzing with the rumor that semen—SEMEN!—had been found in Rod Stewart's tummy. Or was it David Bowie's? And who was looking in these tummies, and how? But adult sexuality was a mishmash and a rumor, like a ridiculous, ominous dirigible that occasionally appeared in the sky, scaring the shit out of us and making us giggle all at once. Anyway, you'd done something—but what, exactly, we did not know. Remember, it was a different time: Rape meant a stranger, an alley, a dark night, a knife at the throat. Anything that went off script was immediately suspect. Sex with a thirteen-year-old is rape, we know now, we say now. But maybe things were not so clear then. They certainly were not clear to you. You fucking moron.

So by the time I was thirteen, your name was known to me, a name that wore devil's horns. By the time I was thirteen, too, I was already used to adult male attention. Even me, with my puff of brown hair and my Trapper Keeper clutched to my chest—men cornered me on the street, breathed on me at parties, yelled at me from cars. I was used to male attention, but I didn't understand it.

I remember being thirteen, the age Samantha Gailey was when you had sex with her, when you fucked her in the ass. I remember lying on the beach by Puget Sound, reading *Pride and Prejudice* and listening to "Ant Music" on my boom box. It was a huge hassle keeping myself in D batteries. I had a shiny Dolphin one-piece swimsuit, a ballpoint-pen drawing of a heart on the instep of my foot, and a giant frizz of hair that I tried to tame, Roseanne Roseannadanna–style, with little clips. My body was narrow, with a child's soft shelf of stomach. When I looked at myself in the mirror from the side, I could see that my stomach stuck out as far as my breasts.

I didn't have a boyfriend, unlike some of the other girls in my class. My coarse, frizzy hair wouldn't feather, and somehow feathered hair seemed to be a prerequisite for having a boyfriend. Not having a boyfriend didn't bother me, at least not usually. I didn't even really think of myself that way; I was still as much kid as I was teenager.

Even so, I wasn't some disembodied *aesthete*. My body felt good to me. I had a trick of making myself feel like a movie star. A classic move: I did it now, on the beach. I lay on my back, one leg extended, the other leg bent at the knee. Sunglasses, of course (Vuarnets purloined from my brother). It was a kind of adult drag I was trying on. I was enjoying the grown-up music, the grown-up book, the grown-up feeling of looking like a seductress. But that didn't mean I was seductive or that I wanted to seduce. These were, insofar as I thought of them at all, terrible words to me: seductress, seductive, seduce. They were the words for someone who must make an effort to be desired. That was not my plan. My plan was to be loved for who I was, for my own self. There would be, when the time came, no need for seduction. I was sure that I myself would prove to be sufficient, when the time came, just like Elizabeth Bennet, who certainly had no need to seduce.

I say on the one hand that I was used to male attention, and on the other hand that I was a kid with a kid's innocence. Does this confuse you, Roman Polanski? Does this make you feel like I deserved whatever I got, or that somehow I was more of a woman, more of a sexual being than I realized? I can tell you that as I lay there like darling Lo, leg bent, sunglasses on, I was just goofing around. I wasn't wishing for sex or even for love. I was perfectly at peace, as the tide came in, washing the almost-transparent bright brown sheaves of seaweed over the barnacled rocks.

I remember being thirteen. It was 1980. There were weird people around all the time. In 1973, my matron mom had left my burgher dad for a hippie eight years her junior. Larry had love beads and hair to his shoulders and a beard so long he could braid it (and, what's more, he did). He had a lot of records: Bob, Van, Neil, the Band, John Sebastian, CSNY, J. J. Cale (the Tulsa

Sound!), Jesse Colin Young, the Flying Burrito Brothers. He had a lot of weed, which we called dope then. He also had a lot of merry, childish friends, men who were like wonderful hairy overgrown kids.

My mother, my brother, Larry, and I all lived during the school year in the house we used to share (except for Larry) with our dad, in a fancy neighborhood on the shore of Lake Washington. In the summer, though, Larry's influence took hold and we lived in a cabin, on a boat, in a chicken coop, and finally in a house we built on a faraway hippie island—no cars, no electricity, no plumbing. Larry ran a tugboat company from there, and sometimes my brother and I deckhanded for him. But mostly we ran wild, wild, wild. We were free enough in Seattle, riding our bikes or taking the bus anywhere we cared to go, but on the island our freedom reached new heights; we disappeared all day long, showed up grimy and half soaked with saltwater at bedtime.

Everywhere we went on that island, my brother and I encountered strange people. (We ourselves were strange people, this proper matron, her two children, and her twenty-something boyfriend.) When we moved to the island, our first friend was named Skeet. He wore a loincloth and fertilized his garden with outhouse gleanings. He had a teenage girlfriend and she was, I think I remember, pregnant. Skeet disappeared quickly, but in his place came more weirdos.

Weirdos everywhere. Not that there was anything wrong with that. They were just people trying to figure out different, original, new ways of living that involved yurts. And they were nice weirdos, mostly. And anyhow, I was used to it. I was used to the smell of pot smoke (though I hated it, with a disgusted rage). I was used to strangers. These people, these sketchy people, came and went in my 1970s. That was part of my mother's freedom, having these weirdos show up and stay for a while.

That was part of the whole deal; it was no longer the thing to hang around with the people *like you*, the people you *grew up with*. The idea was to mix it up, to make your life and even your home more porous, so that new waters could flow through and . . . well, I don't know what. Blow your mind? Get you high? Chat with you?

But that's how things were then, at least for me. What had previously been a fairly contained world—my mother's Irish Catholic milieu, my father's society Seattle milieu—was now expanding. And that was a good thing, wasn't it? Like liberation of all kinds, including sexual liberation, this new social freedom and mobility was a good thing. Wasn't it? For everyone. Well, maybe not for everyone. Maybe not for little girls.

One of these new people appeared as I lay there on the stony beach next to the frigid waters of Puget Sound in July 1980. I lay in repose, in happiness, in freedom, when Jack Wolf strolled up to me. The perpetually high Jack Wolf (he was one of those people always referred to by his full name) wore his hair in a tight brown braid down his back. He had a long, handsome face and downturned, inscrutable eyes.

Jack Wolf was an acquaintance of Larry's. That summer he came to stay with us—for a few days? a weekend?—I think he must have been sleeping on our tugboat at night.

"Hey," said Jack Wolf now. He leaned over me. "What's up with you?"

"Just reading."

"That's cool," said Jack Wolf. He just sat there and looked at me.

My mother was in the house, up a narrow path, on the other side of a small woods. Jack Wolf continued to look at me. He ran his eyes over me. I had read that phrase in a book, and now it was happening to me. The first time I met him, the previous year, at a hippie party at a quasi-commune on a beach near

Seattle, he had led me away from the group, down the beach, and taken a couple of rolls of photos of me, wordlessly. I had been enchanted by his braid and his attention but didn't know how to talk to him.

So it was now. I couldn't think of anything to say. I wanted to impress him—he was one of Larry's friends, after all. Remember this was 1980, which was really still the '70s, and here was this guy kitted out with the signifiers of cool—filthy clothes, long hair, laconic speech, all the stuff I knew to be aces, all the stuff I myself aspired to. I wanted to *be* my brother, to *be* Larry. This is how I wanted to look, to act, an aspiration that would confuse me and cloud my aesthetic for the rest of my life.

We sat in silence until my brother, Dave, appeared and sat down next to Jack Wolf, trying to draw away his gaze, or so it seemed to me.

"Hey," they said to each other.

I got up to walk away. "I'm getting a lemonade," I said nervously.

As I walked away, treading sloppily on the pebbled beach, I heard Jack Wolf say something to my brother. I couldn't hear what. There was a moment of beachy silence: water lapping at the shore, the call of a gull, a hush of wind. And then rocks crunched and squeaked as Dave, lithe and sixteen and fast as a snake, scrambled up from where he sat, ran across the beach to me, and walked me to the house.

Roman Polanski, I'm old now. Old like you. But I remember being thirteen. It was a different time, a time when grown-ups were busy looking for themselves, whatever that meant; a time when kids roamed the countryside and city streets unsupervised; a time when sex had been let off its leash and was loose in the world. There were not so many safety nets for us then.

Even an upper-middle-class kid like me was left much to her own devices, for good or ill.

I remember being thirteen, and so I convince myself that maybe I know what it was like to be Samantha Gailey, who on the evening of March 10, 1977, was just, after all, a thirteen-year-old girl. I can, I tell myself, imagine myself into her predicament. The details are not hard to come by. I deduce her life from court documents, from transcripts, from interviews, from your memoir and from hers. From news reports and offhand comments she has made in the process of declining to be interviewed. I know what I know about her because of her proximity to fame. She was raped by a man with a history, and that has made her own history a matter of record. She has left a trace, unlike most thirteen-year-old girls, who simply disappear into fleshier saggier wiser women.

The 1970s, especially the West Coast in the 1970s, gave rise to a miasmic demimonde, the way geomorphic shapes are thrown up where plates meet. Samantha Gailey and her mother and her sister lived in this demimonde. Not yet fourteen, Samantha was already sexually active. She lived the attenuated, free, overheated life of a young teen girl in the 1970s, of some young teen girls now. But then it was *new*. It was into this life that you walked.

It's not so surprising that you found her. As I've said, strange men flowed into strange places in those times. How did you come to be hanging around the girl Samantha Gailey? You were assigned to take photos of underage models for *Vogue Hommes*. That was the assignment: Take titillating photos of thirteen-year-old girls from around the world. And who gave you this assignment? Well, you pitched it to the magazine yourself.

You and a pal had met Gailey's mom at a cocktail bar on Sunset Strip, where she, an aspiring actress, came on to you. Somehow or another (there's a novel in there) your friend ended up dating Mrs. Gailey's older (relatively speaking; she was only fifteen) daughter. When it came time to shoot the *Vogue Hommes* spread, the friend suggested the younger daughter, thirteen-year-old Samantha, as a likely subject.

Every brick that gets mortared into the story just dizzyingly reiterates this event as emblematic, the ne plus ultra of '70s-ism. For instance: When you went to pick the girl up on the night in question, the mom was relaxing at home with her new boyfriend, who was on the editorial board of *Marijuana Monthly* magazine.

The mom stayed at home while you, Roman Polanski, went to take her daughter's picture—for the second time, in fact. Once before you'd shot Samantha's photo, on the hillside above her house in the Valley. Among the scrub she had posed for you, eventually removing her shirt, a fact she did not tell her mother. (So much *photographing* in the '70s.)

Samantha looked at the contact sheets from the previous shoot as you drove up Mulholland. You pulled in at Jack Nicholson's place (as one does). Here, in my imagination, the events of the evening become a series of static scenes—like a group of depressing, titillating dioramas titled "Life in the 1970s."

When you arrived at the house, a woman with black hair was there to meet you—Nicholson's housesitter. You went to the fridge, pulled out a bottle of champagne, and offered a drink to the girl and the woman.

The housesitter left, and you took some photos of Samantha in the living room. Then you repaired to the bathroom, where you offered her part of a quaalude. It was not her first time taking the drug. In her testimony she would say she'd taken it before "when I was real little." Think about that for a minute, RP. Quaalude successfully introduced into girl, you suggested that the two of you get in the Jacuzzi. Samantha tried to get in wearing her underpants. (Oh! the difficulties of that word.

In the court documents, they're always called panties [and the panties in question were eventually scissored in half by judge's order, that the prosecution might test one half for semen and the defense might test the other]. But "panties" seems gently pornographic, fetishistic, so I'll go with "underpants," despite the word's comic and slightly childish sound.) You chivvied her into nudity and took her picture, in the Jacuzzi, naked. You got in and put your arm around her. She said she had asthma (she didn't) and needed to get out, needed to go home to get her medication. You told her you'd take her home in a bit.

Samantha went into the bathroom to dry off. You followed her and told her to go into the guest cabana. She went where you sent her, thirteen and naked and full of quaalude, and sat down on the couch rather than the bed. You sat down next to her, kissed her, penetrated her, apparently became concerned about birth control, asked her if she was on her period or the pill. When you got a negative to both questions, you made a critical adjustment in angle, penetrated her anally, and—after fending off a knock on the door from Anjelica Huston, who'd popped by—ejaculated in what the girl, in her deposition, heart-breakingly called "my butt."

Samantha Gailey testified she was saying no throughout, though she didn't fight. You have said repeatedly it was con-sensual and noted that the girl was "not unexperienced." This difference in perspective doesn't change the essential fact of the night: You had sex with her. This is one of those stories that can be told in many different ways: You raped her; you date-raped her; you statutory raped her; you made love; you fucked her; it was consensual; it was nonconsensual, even if she never said no, because her very age was like a gag on her. Anyway, you had sex.

.   .   .

What was it like when you came to her on the couch in the cabana? Was she hunched and afraid? Curled up and freaked out? Was she lying there like a Lolita, her knee bent, her head tilted back, in an attitude of innocent, ironic seduction? Maybe you were so worn out by life and its punishments that all you could see was the vague female shape of her. Maybe you were high. Maybe you were bored. Maybe you were angry or frustrated or sad. Maybe you looked at her and saw the same thing you saw everywhere: a hole, the hole that you rushed to fill before it became too scary. I wonder. Maybe you saw what your apologists say you saw: a sexually experienced girl, not much younger than lots of other girls that lots of other men were sleeping with during those fever-dream days.

Perhaps it's significant that I try so hard to view the scene from your point of view. I immediately ask: What did you see when you looked at her? Even I, with my earnest intent to imagine her experience, allow the story to be hijacked by you, Polanski. I've barely begun and I've already failed. Your point of view is the important point of view, the point of view that gives the event historical significance.

This was in fact a meeting of history and non-history, fame and anonymity. You, Polanski, were Western Civ in a Jacuzzi. Your history was large, straddled continents and women. Your mother was gassed at Auschwitz; your father spent years in concentration camps. You raised yourself, became famous for your insanely precocious talent while still in art school, and finally made it to Hollywood only to lose your beloved, beautiful wife and unborn child in one of the most famously grisly murders of the American century. You saw, with your dark, shiny eyes, dark things, and retold them in ways that would make everyone else see the darkness.

It feels *off* to talk about the importance of your work because your movies themselves are so personal, so weird, so unconcerned with posterity and universality and all the other bignesses. We think of beautiful films as being expansive—*Lawrence of Arabia*, *The Last Emperor.* Yours are, there's no denying, perfectly, elegantly composed, but they're also often tight and hot, wrong-way telescoped. Even when you roll through a landscape with a generous bird's-eye view, we can feel we are headed somewhere small and narrow and scary.

Many people have talked about this claustrophobia in terms of your own history. When your parents were sent to the camps, you hid yourself in the Polish countryside; possibly this period in your life was the basis of your friend Jerzy Kosiński's novel *The Painted Bird*. This hiding, people say, explains the closeness of your films: the way the walls close in on Catherine Deneuve in *Repulsion;* the boaty saltwater confines of *Knife in the Water.* But of course people want to explain away all your work in terms of your personal history; it's irresistible because your story is so magnificently tragic. People say the Manson murders formed and knit together with your work: the ultraviolence of your *Macbeth;* the hopelessness of *Chinatown.*

You are undeniably a genius. I wonder: Is your terrible history tied to your genius? Did your history make your work great? Does a genius get let off the hook? Are you great because you're sick? What does it even mean to be a genius? And why are we so willing to call filmmakers geniuses? I suppose because the rest of us—diffident, confused, *female*—can't conceive of setting so many other people in motion in service of our vision. Symphonies and films—these are often called works of genius simply because their makers ask so many other people to *do shit for them.* A genius is, by nature, bossy. He is the boss of the people who work for him, but also the boss of the people who consume his art. The genius—like the alcoholic—overwhelms you with his vision. He requires that you *see things his way.* You walk out of the theater and the world around you looks noticeably different. More brutal, more kind, more filled with light or menace or love or dogs. Whatever the genius fills his movie with.

A boss. That's what you did to Samantha Gailey. You bossed her into your version of how things would go. You made her into a survivor like yourself, something I feel sure she never wanted to be. You put your history all over her, made her take it.

But what about her history? It may be true that you contained the vasty deep of twentieth-century European darkness, but she had a history, too, and cultural forces were also at work on her. In her case, cultural forces involving promiscuity and lack of supervision and the sexualization of children. She embodied all that stuff. Every girl has and is a history.

The summer I was thirteen and living on that cold northern island, I took to sleeping outside. My assigned bedroom was a small open loft I shared with my brother, Dave—I think I knew he wanted his adolescent privacy and so I cleared out. I usually spread my sleeping bag on the porch but that night I laid it on the blond meadow grass, not far from our house. Maybe it was the season of the Perseid showers? That would explain why I was sleeping in the open—to lie on my back and gaze up at the falling sky.

There I lay when Jack Wolf left the house where he'd been drinking and, I'm sure, smoking with my mom and Larry. He walked across the grass toward the path that would lead him down to the beach, where the tugboat's dinghy was tied. He had to walk past me in my sleeping bag, in the dark gray green light, to get where he was going. Or, if he didn't have to, that's what he did anyway. Had I put my sleeping bag there on purpose? Was I hoping he would walk by? Who knows. Did he have intentionality? Did I? Does anything matter except how things turned out?

He stopped and dropped to the grass next to me. Leaned back on his hands and looked up at the stars. "Amazing, huh?"

It's hard to overstate how much I looked up to the young

men Larry brought around. Larry was twenty-four to my mother's thirty-two when he came to live with us. In 1980, Larry would have been just thirty; Jack Wolf was in his twenties. I was thirteen. I worshipped him as quickly and easily as I worshipped my brother.

Anyway he got in the sleeping bag with me, and opened my mouth, and put a lump of hash in, like the pill that is administered to Mia Farrow at the end of *Rosemary's Baby*. I think that's the order of what happened. Somewhere in there he gave me the hash; somewhere in there he got in the bag. I lay there with the stuff on my tongue and felt him next to me, pressing against me. He wasn't there very long, maybe minutes? Maybe seconds? I felt something pressing, repeatedly, against my naked thigh. That's all it was, no big deal, just something rubbing, rubbing against me.

Those islands are far from anyplace. The silence there is the kind of silence that has dozens of miles of other silence surrounding it. You're vulnerable to the ordinary: A moonrise, the call of an owl can disrupt your equilibrium. Disequilibrium. It's strange to think that a darkness more dark, a silence more silent, a peace more absolute could seem fragile. For of course in daily life, in town and in the city, we're used to incursions; they hardly matter. They are in fact the very stuff of life. But in the absolute silence and the total dark, an incursion, however tiny, is frightening and awesome and terrible. A pinecone falls, etc. Well, you know, Roman Polanski.

I heard my mother's voice call from the porch: "Claire! Good night!" The sound of her voice sent the hippie out of my sleeping bag and away through the night.

When I say I can imagine myself into Samantha Gailey's predicament, when I place my small story next to hers, am I stealing something that doesn't belong to me? After all, there is a kind of terrible hierarchy of abuse. I don't want to co-opt Samantha Gailey's experience. But I can't help thinking of her story as a kind of parable. Don't get me wrong, I know it was real enough for her.

Even so, hers was an extreme version of something that so many of us went through.

The next morning my brother and I were on the porch. I was reading; he was sitting on the floor, leaning against the wall of the house, absently and obsessively strumming his guitar with his usual absent-eyed, idiot guitar face. Of course on him it looked cool. A mug of coffee, an affectation he'd recently picked up, sat on the floor next to him.

Reid Harbor sparkled in the sun below us. I didn't know it at the time, but we were beautiful children: our matching cheekbones and modeled chins, Dave's sea-green eyes and my murkier hazel; the orange peel curling at my elbow on the picnic table, sweating its fragrant oil in the sun; our good teeth, our educations, our straight backs and strong legs. It all spoke of ease and a kind of blessedness. There was nothing malodorous there, just the smell of saltwater and orange. But our very freedom meant that we were imperfectly protected, and David knew it. He wanted to tell me he would protect me, whether I liked it or not.

He looked at me with narrow eyes and stopped strumming.

"Jack Wolf is a dick," he said.

Huh? Did David really know everything? Everything on earth? I reddened. Blushing is too nice a word for what I did; blushing sounds maidenly. Austen-ly. This was brick-red shame.

"Yeah, he does seem like kind of a dick," I said.

"You want to know what he said to me yesterday?" He began

strumming again and dropped his head, looking slightly to his left at his fingers on the fretboard.

"What?" I asked, though in fact I did not want to know.

"He said, 'I bet your sister has a sweet box.'"

"Oh." I didn't say, What's a box? Or, Why would it be sweet? Or, Why are you telling me this?

David rolled his weight forward onto his feet, and stood up, and went into the house. We never spoke of it again.

Samantha Gailey knew what she had, maybe. She'd begun having sex the previous year, as did so many girls of that era—and in fact this became one of your standard lines when defending yourself to the press: the girl's "experience." She wanted to be in pictures, like her mom. Maybe she wanted to use her power, a little bit. Some people said she was more than opportunistic. Gore Vidal called Samantha a "hooker" in the pages of *The Atlantic*, in the voice of the purest most cynical cronyism: "Look, am I going to sit and weep every time a young hooker feels she's been taken advantage of?"

At any rate, there's a chance that she knew she had some power, some sexual pull. And in just a year, I would know too. The next year I had a bikini and a tan and kept my hair brushed, and when I was deckhanding on the tugboat we always had plenty of volunteers to help out.

But that summer, the summer of Jack Wolf, I had no clue. I was a child. I had no mental game around sex. I wasn't yet an agent or a subject of desire. I was just myself. The relationship between the outside world and myself was uncomplicated and occasionally even porous. I was much given to gape-mouthed reveries and unbrushed hair.

The next year I would be female—affecting the world through gesture, through touch. I would never be able to go back. I would be trapped in a new world, where I wanted and intended to seduce. Was it Jack Wolf's fault? Of course not. It was the fault of time, and the era, and myself. But I do know that I was, as the years went on, going to grow very, very weary of this sexual self, the girl who saw every question as a sex question because that was the only answer she thought she had.

May 17, 1990, age twenty-three

My face is nice when illuminated by love
and just so sad when not.

8

The Love Square: A Cautionary Tale

When I was growing up, my brother and I had adjacent bedrooms. Just beyond our rooms lay a sunlit landing called the Love Square. If you stepped in the Love Square, it meant you were in love. This was not considered a good thing. In fact, being in love was the absolute worst condition possible. The nadir of existence. This was the solemn opinion of my older brother, the inventor of the Love Square.

It was possible to get to the very top of the stairs without putting your foot in the Love Square. You had to sort of diagonally hop around and over it. A lot of time and energy was expended avoiding the Love Square, or tricking visitors into standing in it. Even my mom was careful not to step in it.

My brother jumped over the square with glee; no love for him! I was more ambivalent. Though a squad of torturers couldn't have gotten me to confess it, I sort of *wanted* to stand in the Love Square. I wanted to stand there and see what would happen.

Maybe my mom did accidentally step in the Love Square, because here's what happened: She fell in love. The person she fell in love with was a hippie eight years younger than herself. The timeline of what happened is confusing. When did she leave my dad? When did Larry the hippie move in?

I loved Larry, but I hated the idea of my mom being in love. The original thing I didn't want to think about. Many children hate love. Probably it can be boiled down to an evolutionarily developed aversion to sex before one is physically ready to reproduce. Gross! But sometimes I think it's just because love leaves children out. Love means the adults are busying themselves elsewhere. Love is a distracted mother, who's kissing not you but someone else. That's annoying even if it's your father, let alone some hippie. Moms are supposed to be frickin' *on tap*.

Anyway in 1973 my dad moved out and my mom's young hippie boyfriend Larry moved in. I missed my dad, but I loved Larry right from the start. From my point of view, my dad's departure had nothing whatsoever to do with Larry, whom I saw as a kind of divinely fun, infinitely tolerant older brother.

It was never a bad thing that Larry moved in, but it was sort of a *weird* thing. We lived in Laurelhurst, a staid, fancy neighborhood near the lake, green with the eponymous laurel and rhododendron and Douglas fir. It seemed to me, little as I was, that most people in Laurelhurst didn't have hippies turning up in their houses. (How wrong I was.) So when Mrs. Rose—a neighbor, the mother of my playmate Joni, set-haired matron, probable Republican—asked me who was that strange man she kept seeing around our house, I answered, quick as a bunny, "He's the handyman. He sleeps over the garage." Even though I was only six years old, note how I got straight to the heart of the matter: WHERE WAS HE SLEEPING? How did I know this was the crux of the thing? And how on earth did I come up with "over the garage"? There *was* no "over the garage." But I was trying to protect everyone: my mom, Larry, Mrs. Rose, myself. That Mrs. Rose and I shared a distaste for extramarital physical love was a truth I grasped instinctively.

The genius of Larry was that he found a way to let me and Dave into his love. For instance, my brother found out that Elton John, his favorite musician, was going to be on TV. This was great news. In those days of course it was very rare to have the chance to see your favorite performer on television. The closest you usually got to live footage was wiggling the album cover while listening to the music.

I expected Dave to be happy, but once he told me the news, he began to look dejected. We stood in the den together. He pointed at our TV.

"The problem," he said, "is *that*."

"Is what?"

"Is that TV."

"Why?"

"Because, duh. It's a black-and-white. We have to see Elton John in color. He's probably the most colorful person in the world."

Our mother came in. Now we were both dejected. We explained the situation. She probably lit up a cigarette, I can't remember. "Well," she said. "Too bad."

It was a dark day. When Dave was sad, I was sad. I liked having my brother near me, or needed it. I felt most alive when he looked at me with his clear, skeptical green eyes. I would do anything to get him to notice me. He, forceful and full of ideas, made the world as he thought it should be, and I joined in. The stuff my brother thought up to do—jumping off the bulkhead into the rocky sand below, riding Big Wheels down the steep hill behind our house, climbing the tallest tree at the playground— was stuff he, strong and wiry and, well, boyish, was built for. I, soft and spacey, was made for something else but didn't even know there *was* anything else. So I did my best to be exactly like him. It wasn't just that I was a tomboy, though that is a convenient word for what I was. I was, in fact, a romantic—a girl entirely in love with her big brother. If I could somehow have trained my body to grow up just like his, I would've done it gladly, out of love and hero worship and the profound abasement that informed my daily life with this god.

Finally Larry came home from the water-ski factory where he worked. It was after five.

"What's wrong?" he asked, lying down on the couch in the den, looking like he was thinking about lighting up a number, as he called it.

We explained again. My mom went into the kitchen to work on dinner. Larry hopped up, went into the kitchen, got the newspaper, turned to the classifieds section, and grabbed a pen. He began to circle things. It's quite a landscape, if you think about it: this kid, with his long hair and greasy jeans, sitting at a nice telephone table in the nice wallpapered kitchen of this nice ivy-covered house in nice leafy Laurelhurst. It still sort of blows my mind. Anyway, he dialed (oh yes) the phone, had a brief exchange with someone on the other end. "We'll be there in half an hour," he said, and hung up.

"Okay, we've got to drive down to Renton," he said.

"What?" I asked. "Why?"

"We're gonna buy a color TV."

My mom started laughing. "What about dinner?"

"Let's go!" said Larry. "Elton John is gonna be on in an hour and a half."

We loaded into his Econoline van. It was already dark out. Mom had turned off the electric frying pan in the middle of cooking dinner. It was all too much!

Renton was far away—would we make it in time? Larry went hell for leather. Dave and I bounced around in the back of the van—there were no seats. My mom smoked cigarette after cigarette.

We pulled up to a little house and were greeted by a man. We all crowded into the garage, where he switched on the TV to prove that it worked.

"Great!" said Larry. "We'll take it." He took a wad of money out of the front pocket of his 501s and began peeling off bills.

"Don't you want to check all the channels, or something?" Larry's speed seemed to be freaking the man out.

"Good idea. Dave, what channel is your show on?"

Dave clicked the dial to the right channel and it did indeed come through fine.

Larry hoisted the TV and we all but ran to the van. Dave slid open its heavy door and the TV was ours. We barreled home through the night.

The color of Elton John was sky blue. He was positively swathed in it. He wore a sky-blue suit, a sky-blue feather boa, sky-blue shoes, and enormous sky-blue sunglasses. As if to reward us for our drive to Renton, the TV gave us a surfeit of sky-blue Elton Johns: His image in the center of the screen was surrounded by smaller Elton Johns, the way a large diamond (or, I suppose, a sapphire) might be set in a circlet of smaller gems. We sat on the floor in front of the TV, rapt, dazzled. David was satisfied, and so I was too.

Larry watched us watching. And I don't remember this, but I bet my mom watched Larry. That is what I would have done if I were her and someone had just declared his love for me in this particular way.

One morning when I was in maybe first grade, I decided to try it. I knew I was safe: Dave was outside playing, Larry was at work, my mom was in the basement doing laundry. I solemnly approached the Love Square. Set one foot down. Then the other. Stood there. It was a lonely feeling, being the only one in the house who would abase herself enough to wish for love, to stand still for moments on end in that shameful, shag-carpeted spot. I kept standing there, waiting for love, so terrible, to come and change me. Nothing. Motes drifted.

February 4, 1981, age fourteen

I rode home on the bus with Sam, but I don't really like him excessively anymore. He's too chicken to do anything, anyway.

9

Josephine in Laurelhurst

Late one hot night in August 1980 I draped myself over the plaid armchair in the den, as though my body were a burden I was trying to cast off. There was nothing on TV, but I gazed blankly at it anyway. Behind the TV was a bookcase. This particular bookcase had long been depleted of all its goodness. At age thirteen, I felt I'd located and consumed anything of value there. I had found the dirty books (*Fear of Flying*) and the funny books (*My World and Welcome to It*) and the books with young girls as narrators (*A Member of the Wedding*). Now the shelves were fruit sucked dry. Only the pips were left: *The Forsyte Saga*. *Hawaii. Trask.* I had tried John Updike's Rabbit books and Annie Dillard's *Pilgrim at Tinker Creek* and John Cheever's *The World of Apples*—books with titles so beautiful they practically glowed, but whose insides disappointed when you actually tried to read them. Where were the apples? The rabbits?

A title now jumped out at me: *Taps at Reveille*, F. Scott Fitzgerald, the words running down the spine in a fat friendly-looking serif typeface. I'd always skipped over the book in the past because it sounded—ugh—military. But now I was so bored that the typeface was enough to pull me from my chair to the shelf. The first story, "The Scandal Detectives," told about a boy in a small town at the turn of the century—my favorite setting for fiction—wreaking havoc on his contemporaries with naughty tricks. And yet here it was in a volume of what was clearly serious literature. It was almost too good to be true.

What I'd stumbled upon were the Basil and Josephine stories, parallel suites of coming-of-age stories about Basil, a boy much like Fitzgerald, and Josephine, a girl based on Fitzgerald's real-life early love Ginevra King. Basil and Josephine never meet, but their stories run along next to each other like gleaming train tracks. Their destined meeting is the rich eggy center of the stories, implied and never stated. The boy, Basil, is callow, egotistical, sensitive, prone to showing off. The girl, Josephine, is manipulative, selfish, romantic, and forever getting in trouble for being fast. Both are total fuckups and both are built for love; this much is obvious from the opening pages of the first story I read, where fourteen-year-old Basil savors the coming of night: "It was five o'clock and there was a small crowd gathered there for that soft and romantic time before supper—a time surpassed only by the interim of summer dusk thereafter."

I read all the stories (at least all that were gathered in *Taps at Reveille;* there are more) in a go that first night; I was up until dawn. Like Basil, like Josephine, I was subject to the unspeakable glamour of the night. Basil was sort of familiar-seeming—in fact, he elicited in me *exactly* the feeling I used to have when my brother and I would watch *Leave It to Beaver* and we knew the Beav was going to get in trouble and it would upset us so much that we would climb behind the black Naugahyde couch and watch from there.

Josephine was another story. She seemed magical and terrible and fallible in a way that upset me deeply, and that I loved. I would list here the different plots of the Josephine stories except that they were all rather similar. The first story in the series is typical: Sixteen-year-old Josephine throws herself headlong at a twenty-two-year-old college man, Anthony Harker. When she succeeds in making him fall in love with her, she promptly dumps him, leaving him heartbroken and also marked forever as a pervy suitor of teenage girls. At the end of the story, Harker asks her why she did it, and Fitzgerald sums up the major theme of the Josephine stories: "There would have been no use saying the simple truth—that she could not help what she had done, that great beauty has a need, almost an obligation, of trying itself, and that her ample cup of emotion had spilled over on its own accord, and it was an accident that it had destroyed him and not her."

The stories follow Josephine as again and again she administers this test of her own beauty; her only interest is making men fall in love with her. It's her vocation. "She was an egotist who played not for popularity but for individual men."

I knew a word for what Josephine was: a slut. But of course in her day they had something a little nicer: A girl like Josephine was fast, or a speed. She confesses that she's "Just sort of speedy—you know, sort of pash." Josephine is someone hurtling forward into the future; she is, as Fitzgerald sees her, a new kind of person, a person in a hurry to get somewhere, emotionally and sexually speaking. The problem is, whenever she gets there, she loses interest in what she has just attained. In pursuit of her ever-receding destination, story after story finds Josephine zeroing in on some boy—or, increasingly, man—whose appeal is occasionally seemingly random. And she seems to know it. In "A Nice Quiet Place," she determinedly falls in love with a boy she sees walking past her window: "But she could have cared for almost anyone. She wanted to hear the mystical terminology of love, to feel the lift and pull inside herself that each one of a dozen affairs had given her."

I picture myself sprawling all thirteen-like on the plaid chair, getting up for more Ritz crackers or grapes, turning the pages in a state of total absorption. I *hated* Josephine! She was horrid. My sympathies were with the boy victims. And yet there was something I saw in her that even then I recognized. Not that I was or ever would be a great beauty—at this time I was a hunching beanpole with waist-length hair full of knots and tangles—but Josephine's desire to take hold of a male was something I understood very well, with all the passion of a younger sister.

When I first read the Basil and Josephine stories, I had never fallen in love. I had known boys I suspected were soul mates—Tommy Halvorsen, for instance, with whom I walked to advanced reading in the portables in first and second grade; a boy named Christian who had three apple trees in his yard and earnestly forced the Earthsea Trilogy on me—but I was too little for love. And I'd always been too funny-looking for it besides.

I had been a tomboy, or tried to be one, for so many years. Tried to keep up with my brother as well as I could. Being a tomboy was supposed to be daring, but it was the safest thing to be when I was a kid. It kept the world off your back. You weren't vulnerable, the way a girl was. I spent my time trying to be near boys, or trying to be a boy. Tomboys ran—wild as ponies— across the landscape of the 1970s: Tatum O'Neal, Jodie Foster, Kristy McNichol, Melissa Gilbert. No one wanted to be Mary; everyone wanted to be Laura. Girls were beneath contempt. For instance: Eleanor Lund, who lived up the hill from me. She wore dresses. And she didn't even wear gym shorts underneath them, just underpants. She hated it when we swore. One day we were playing in Eleanor Lund's yard—good swing set—and I was making fun of another kid for farting. I'm not proud of it. I said something clever like, "Hey! You farted." Eleanor Lund swept over and said imperiously, "*We* call them windies and *we* don't think they're funny." It became a catchphrase among me and my family. We scorned Eleanor Lund; her crime was that she was a girl, inescapably a girl. It was as if she were some kind of transference object. Her immaculate femininity became a receptacle for our self-loathing. I myself liked to march around in cutoffs and a hoodie and was proud when a grown-up called me boy.

But, secretly, I sensed in myself a lovable destiny. And it was true. Only a year later I began a career of adherence to Josephine's scattershot methodology: I could care for almost anyone, and often make them care for me.

Is this what happens to every girl who secretly believes she's a boy, or at least fervently wishes to be one? What happens when she gets older and the very machine of her turns out to be soft and round rather than hard and narrow? Belief can't stop those things from happening. An interior sense of who you are, of who you ought to be—the body, the machine, doesn't listen to these things. The machine is built to go in only one direction: forward. It doesn't give a shit what its passenger is thinking. This betrayal by the body is every adolescent's story. In my case, it brought me up against the truth. I would never be my brother. I would never be the special kind of inviolable—just say it, the special kind of superior—that boys are. I would be imperfect. I would be a girl. There was no pretending any longer, once the boobs came. And yet: I still thought boys were best. I knew it. It was in this state of realizing my own essential imperfection that I began to look for love; like Josephine, I fixed my sights on someone and made him mine. Over and over.

My gaze fell first on Sam, a childhood playmate and the only boy I knew who'd read L. M. Montgomery. Sam and I were part of a group of eighth-graders who volubly and almost professionally loved the Beatles: me, Sam, Ben, Janie, and the other Ben. Any album was acceptable, but especially important to us were *Rubber Soul* and *Revolver*. It was the dawn of the '80s, but we just wanted to escape into the black-and-white world of the moptops. There was something about the cultural moment when the hair hit the shirt collar that moved us: a safe rebellion. And so when *A Hard Day's Night* showed at the Market Cinema, off we all trooped to see it, even though it was a school night. No VCRs is why.

The evening was organized around me and Sam—his friends made sure he was next to me, my friends made sure I was next to him, and the seating plan radiated outward from there. I was almost fourteen years old. Something had changed. Maybe it was just that I had started parting my hair differently: on the side, elegant, rather than in the middle, dorky. A doughiness had fallen from my face. I was very tall, one of the tallest kids in my grade. And now I had a boyfriend. I told his best friend I liked him; he told my best friend he liked me; and so the deal was brokered. Sam and I sat in the center of the row of kids in that musty movie theater, and we were, for a moment, at the center of the world. We giggled and poked, except Ben, who was the most serious of us about the Beatles. A flickering outage of the lights and a raising of the curtain and there we were in the dark.

I set my hand on the armrest between me and Sam, available. I hadn't known until this exact moment what I wanted, hadn't thought about wanting anything at all, but now I wanted this: I wanted him to take my hand. Here I was, seeing the film I'd longed to see, and all I could think of was my untended paw. I sat in a roil, as the Beatles wound up the reporters, the designated grown-ups of the film:

REPORTER: How did you find America?
JOHN: Turned left at Greenland.
REPORTER: Are you a mod or a rocker?
RINGO: Um, no. I'm a mocker.

I let my hand lay there on the armrest. I sort of let it dangle off the edge, suggestively, I hoped.

REPORTER: What would you call that hairstyle you're
    wearing?
GEORGE: Arthur.

I squirmed in my seat. It was very hard to concentrate. The
moptops unfurled their tightly controlled ironies on the screen,
so blunt and funny and unemotional.

REPORTER: Do you often see your father?
PAUL: No, actually, we're just good friends.

Somehow Sam was now aligned with the Beatles, with
restraint, with irony, while I was all messy desire. I began to feel
embarrassed. There I was, waiting. There was my hand, which
had come to seem an almost disembodied thing. Did he not
want it? Was he against hand-holding? Was there something
wrong with me for wanting him to hold it (likeliest scenario)?
I was hurt, but also kind of pissed. Why couldn't I get what I
wanted? It didn't matter that he "liked" me; I wanted him to
touch me.

In other words: The moment I entered sexual and romantic
life, as one walking through a gate, I learned that I wanted more.
I learned that I operated at a higher pitch, sexually and romantically, than other people. I wanted harder than other people. And
yet I felt disempowered to take action. I needed someone to do
it *to* me. This need would never go away, though I didn't know
it at the time—I felt this need years later, when my husband
pinned my hands over my head, when the Californian short-
story writer pulled me away from the party.

The film ended and we all got up and bustled and chatted
and laughed. Sam and I didn't meet each other's eye.

.   .   .

After that, it was *on*. I fell, like Josephine, often and disastrously. I didn't care how it turned out, for me or him or anyone else. And I found that, indeed, almost anyone would do. Like Josephine, my list just got longer and longer. And, like Josephine, throughout the seemingly interminable high-school era, I tried to interest myself in other things, but in truth all I wanted was the repeated "lift and pull," over and over, world without end, amen. A boy made the future disappear and now there was only me and him. I *meant* to become interested in other things. I did some of my homework. I wrote poems, or poem-shaped objects. I liked Latin; the linear movement of the language did something restful to my brain, and Pompeii was cool to learn about. I worked on the newspaper and the literary mag and I tried to learn modern Greek. I tried. But really I was pretending. Really I was made for only this one thing.

Josephine tried too. Over and over in the stories, she resolves to change: "She would be a good girl now forever, see less of boys, as her parents wished . . . But the first stars were out over Lake Shore Drive, and all about her she could feel Chicago swinging around its circle at a hundred miles an hour, and Josephine knew that she only wanted to want such wants for her soul's sake. Actually, she had no desire for achievement."

I too had no true desire for achievement. I mean, I planned to write a book one day that would make other people unhappy by its sheer greatness, but mostly I wanted to drive cute boys around in my Dodge Dart listening to oldies on the AM radio underneath the first stars over Lake Washington, and then maybe drink a forty, and then find somewhere secret to go and have sex with the person of the moment. I wanted nothing else. I was, you know, sort of pash.

. . .

A certain numbing could come with all this dispersing of my affections, a numbing of which I was not unaware, nor was Josephine, who asks one of her beaux in "A Woman with a Past": "What's the matter with me? . . . For months I've felt as if I were a hundred years old, and I'm just seventeen . . ."

Exactly such dark misgivings visited me at exactly the same age. I wrote in my diary:

> *July 17, 1983: Lately I have been feeling so old, so used up, burned out. I know that's foolish and a sure sign of youth. I mean, there's this attractive (if a bit pretentious) boy from California here on the island and I could probably have something with him and I'm not interested. The most depressing part is that I feel sort of sure I could "have him." In a way, now, I understand why I was advised not to have sex—now I have nothing to explore there. I understand there are other ways of making love than I have tried and these can be explored—it's just the actual rite of being in a bed with a male. I can't let dissatisfaction creep in. I hate the thought that I might need something which can only be provided by another human.*

But the misgivings didn't mean I changed my behavior, just that I hated myself as I did it. In fact, it grew worse as I entered college and then dropped out; worse because without the structure of family and school, I became buffeted by love. Boys led me from one end of the earth to the other, and I succumbed utterly to what seemed to me the primary and undeniable needs of my emotional life.

There is a final Josephine story, uncollected in *Taps at Reveille*. Titled "Emotional Bankruptcy," it gives us Josephine at nearly eighteen and in love at last; she's met her match in Edward Dicer, the perfect ideal of manhood. Practiced as ever, she of course makes him fall in love with her, and then, when he kisses her, discovers she feels . . . nothing. The story ends with poor little Josephine in a maudlin heap on the couch: "The love of her life had come by, and looking in her empty basket, she had found not a flower left for him—not one. After a while she wept. 'Oh what have I done to myself?' she wailed. 'What have I done?'"

When I first read this, as a teenager, I thought it a very serious business. Josephine left with an empty basket; how awful! "All the old things are true," writes Fitzgerald (even though he's forever telling us that all the new things are true). "One cannot both spend and have." And I, foolish girl, believed him. I was washed up, and so was Josephine. I mean, it wasn't going to affect my *behavior* in any way, but it was very sad.

Sitting in my little studio, an adult, rereading the Josephine tales in one great gulp, I saw things a little differently. The scene now seemed to me the punitive moralizing of a self-hating alcoholic—Josephine *c'est moi*, Fitzgerald is saying. The story is of course about his own emotional bankruptcy, the topic that consumed his later years. But how nasty to visit it upon this little girl whose only sin was liking to kiss a lot of people!

Now, a grown woman, I found myself wondering: What *happened* to Josephine when she found her basket empty? What did she *do*? Did she just lie collapsed on the couch for the rest of her days? Of course Fitzgerald's point is that a creature of emotion is nothing once emotion has died, which is a nice point—but no one is simply a creature of emotion. Not Josephine, not me. For people like Josephine and me, the death of emotion means not the end of life but its beginning; finally we are loosed—ruefully, reluctantly—from the grip of what we've been calling love.

That's how it was for me, or how it was for me for many years. Once I got over the obsessive love-affair-having of my youth, I felt at long last able to turn my attention to more important things: my career, my family.

So why, when I closed my book, did I find myself compulsively drawn to check my e-mail? I actively resisted the urge to rise from my studio armchair where I'd been sprawled in a slightly achy approximation of my thirteen-year-old self. I was determined not to check, not to be preoccupied by a boy, a man. I ate a cookie and read a couple of pages of the introduction to the Basil and Josephine collection. Finally, ever so nonchalantly, I went over to my desk and opened my laptop. There in my little mouse-smelling office, I was Josephine again, testing my pull.

November 11, 1982, age fifteen

I'm sick of all these boring preppies!

10

Scratch a Punk, Find a Hippie

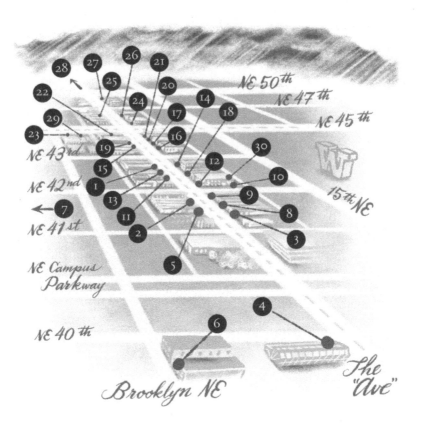

A Selective, Incomplete, Annotated Map of
Seattle's University Way from 1981 to 1985—
That Is, My High-School Years

Scratch a Punk, Find a Hippie

Key

1. PIZZA HAVEN

It seemed like all the dishwashers at Pizza Haven were heavy-metal guitarists. Either in spite of or because of this, no one I knew ever ate here or even walked in the door.

2. KINKO'S

Mission control for Seattle punk rock during the era when flyers were social media. Photocopying was the critical technology of our ethos. Everyone worked here, including Victoria, whom I didn't know at the time.

3. LA TIENDA

Where we bought things to decorate ourselves. The back room was paved in loose bricks and you'd teeter across them to the jewelry cases, where the Mexican earrings were sized big, bigger, biggest. Which was how we liked earrings in the '80s, even punks and mods and hippies like us. (Sometimes we didn't know which of the above we actually were.)

4. ARNOLD'S

Arcade where Vanessa and I played video games and pinball after school, hopped up on espressos. She beat me at Centipede, every single game, four years running.

5. MUFFIN BREAK

The chocolate-chip muffin was the size of your head and would feed you all day, if you augmented it with free coffee from your workplace and beer you begged off some boy.

6. THE LAST EXIT

One sunny afternoon I was sitting alone at a marble table at the Last Exit, drinking an espresso float and waiting to meet a friend. Of course a sixteen-year-old girl couldn't sit alone in a place like that for long, and soon enough a very grubby boy of twenty or so sat down and started talking to me. He smelled of clove cigarettes. After we chatted for a bit he asked where I lived. "Oh, on the other side of the university," I answered airily, which was true but also cagey. I was politician-careful not to use the word Laurelhurst—which was, after all, what lay on the other side of the university. My hair was unbrushed, my jeans and shoes were riddled with holes, I wasn't too clean. My interlocutor didn't miss a beat. "Oh, what part of *Laurelhurst* do you live in?" he asked nastily, and justifiably. I gave him my number and we ended up going out for coffee a couple of times but never had sex or even made out, I'm sure due to some oversight on my part.

The Last Exit was staffed by a team of handsome, twenty-something men with lax morals, and I liked to lure them into my teen love trap. I collected them.

Many years later, as a forty-six-year-old, I encountered one of these guys. I was at a party with my husband, the kind of party we almost never went to anymore, the kind with drugs and a keg and the possibility that someone was going to punch someone else. The din was nearly intolerable. People were *smoking inside.* You could tell you were in Seattle because no one wore any colors and everyone was saying something blandly wicked. The people at this party were denizens of the Ave of my youth. Most of us had known one another for decades. When you greeted someone at this party, you didn't say hello, you said the person's name, drawn out with tender irony, as if you were encompassing everything you knew about him in those syllables—"*Miiiiichaaaael!*"—and then you hugged and laughed.

I was sitting on my husband's lap, chatting/yelling with our hostess, when I sensed I was being observed. I looked up and saw a man staring at me. He was tall, good-looking, maybe ten or twenty years older than me (who can tell anymore?), and he was nearly maroon with embarrassment. I had never seen a grown man blush so hard. Immediately I knew who he was, even though I hadn't laid eyes on him since I was sixteen. Without hesitation, I got up and went over to him and stuck my hand out to be shaken.

"I'm Claire," I said.

"Oh, I know who you are," he said.

We stared at each other speechless, both of us thinking about the dirty things we did to each other when I was a teenager in a beret and he a grown man I met at the Last Exit. I drew closer to him. I didn't want to fuck him; I wanted to interview him. I wanted to say: Tell me everything about what we did, about who I was. Maybe he could explain to me what on earth I was thinking, all those years ago on the Ave.

7. MORNINGTOWN PIZZA

Amazingly, even grimier than the Last Exit. But my guess is you're going to get a lot of grime in any collectively run pizzeria. My brother dropped out of college and got a job here, or became a communard or whatever you want to call it. He joined up.

One day he and I were drinking herbal tea, hibiscus flowers and chamomile, and a Grateful Dead song came on. Filthy hippie girl at the next table said, "Take me away, Uncle Jerry," and Dave and I were laughing so hard we had to leave the restaurant.

It was in the parking lot at Morningtown that I went into the van of J, a creepy homeless hippie guy in his mid-twenties. I mean, I suppose if you count the van he wasn't technically homeless. The windows were hung with Indian-print bedspreads. We never did it, but he kissed me and felt me up in his diesel-smelling van. His mustached mouth reminded me of a vagina. When he went down on me I thought, unbidden, "sideways vagina." Jesus, just the fact that he *had* a mustache is totally humiliating.

8. BULLDOG NEWS

My first real job. My assigned task was to sit in the window like an Amsterdam whore and sell coffee to passersby. Or they came into the shop and bought expensive, artsy European magazines. Fuck yeah! It didn't get any better than that for a pretentious boy-crazy chick in 1985. The most important magazines—aside from *Thrasher,* obviously—were the British style and music rags *The Face* and *i-D.* When I was a kid growing up in Seattle, which was still a profoundly provincial city, the capital we looked toward was not New York but London. London was the place where everything was happening. We kept up with *NME.* We knew what the new Rough Trade releases were. There were a lot of kids going back and forth to London during that time, including Vic. They would fly over there with no plan and live in squats and learn how the Tube worked and join bands and come home and go back again. (This Seattle–London pipeline is perhaps underestimated in the written histories of how Seattle became an important music city.) New York was for dumb people who wanted to take cocaine. We were smart people who wanted to take heroin. So I sold a lot of British magazines.

I had the coveted afternoon shift. Sunlight poured into the west-facing window, illuminating the gray Ave and its indigent denizens. I drank mocha after mocha, reading about English pop stars and wondering if I should crop my hair. My thousands of regulars came by for their drinks and there was banter. At the end of my shift I would close out the till, which was always a scary moment. We had an antique register that did no math on your behalf—like a stern algebra teacher, it made you figure it out yourself—so I had to count people's change back to them the old-fashioned way: twenty-four cents makes three and two dollars makes five. This was fun in a sort of interactive performative way, but scary when it came time to tot up the day's sales. After I'd faced the till, I would dump the tip jar into my giant black leather satchel (I never had anything so practical and bourgeois as a wallet) and motor up to Dick's Drive-In on Forty-fifth and use my tip money to buy my dinner of a hamburger ($.75) with extra ketchup ($.05).

I knew the coffee order of, seemingly, everyone on the Ave. To this day there are people I see around town, and without even knowing their name, I'll think "doppio espresso" or whatever.

9. COFFEE CORRAL

Classic diner with hideous food. Prime location at the corner of Forty-second and the Ave. Vanessa's street pals, who belonged to a punkish-arty gang called the Bag Philosophy Team, the point of which I never understood, hung out here.

10. MAGUS BOOKS

Perfect university-adjacent used-book store. When I say "perfect," here is what I mean: My husband recently texted me a photo of the current window display, which contained *The Basic Writings of Trotsky; I and Thou* by Martin Buber; *Erotism* by Georges Bataille; *The Twentieth Century: A People's History* by Howard Zinn; *Education for Critical Consciousness* by Paulo Freire; something or other by Rollo May. This display has not changed in any meaningful way since I was a child of fourteen, though I suppose the actual books have come and gone.

11. BEAUTY AND THE BOOK

A darkly baroque, extremely grubby bookstore owned by a grizzled roué who hired only beautiful young women. It was said he was sleeping with all of them—how'd he pull *that* off? They sat behind the counter looking ineffectual and sleepy-eyed— maybe he fed them opium? Anyway it was known as a great place for shoplifting.

12. ROXY MUSIC RECORDS
(AND ALSO THE RECORD STORE ACROSS THE STREET)

Flipping through records was something to do with yourself when you didn't know what else to do with yourself. Maybe you took the bus up to the Ave and walked around for a while, looking for a friend or looking to get picked up by a new friend. And nothing happened, not that day, so you went and flipped the bins, your fingers seeming to possess their own brains, feeling each album's weight, looking for who knows what.

13. SIR PLUS

Military thrift stores were where we got almost all of our clothes. In the '80s it was difficult to find anything *plain* enough. Sir Plus had army jackets, Converse high-tops, and, coming into fashion a little later, Bundeswehr tanks.

14. THE WALL

When I was a little kid, the hippies hung out a block away on Fifteenth Ave, on the grass verge called Hippie Hill. Now, driven by the same impulse to gather, sit, look cool, mock, hatch plans, and, well, buy drugs, the punks lined up on the wall by the post office. You didn't walk on that side of the street, mostly. The Bopo Boys ruled everything—first they were a skate gang, then a bad band. My friend Tim claims there was a nice Bopo.

15. NORDSTROM PLACE TWO

Outpost of the downtown department store. Mostly for sorority girls, but notable as a place to buy both kinds of Levi's: shrink-to-fit 501s, and black.

16. SHIGA'S IMPORTS

Source for Chinese flats. Crucial. Worn by all girls, from punks to mods to hippies to preppies. They cost $7.99 and sometimes you could get them in colors, or embroidered. Shiga's was also a supplier of Japanese farmer pants, the official leg-wear of 1985. We were pan-Asian from the waist down.

17. UNIVERSITY BOOK STORE

Safe zone. Time out. Maybe you might run into your mom.

18. SPOONMAN

Artis the Spoonman was later immortalized in a Soundgarden song. He plied his trade on the Ave. He also used to come sit around on the walking path at my prep school, whacking himself all over with spoons.

19. TOWER RECORDS

Many, many people who went on to have big music and/or music-industry careers worked here, and they were all good to look at and funny and way smarter than you. It was where the cutest boys worked, the boys who looked like young Bob Dylan. One of my boyfriends, a drummer named Darren, worked here, and his particular brand of contemptuous reserve was very effective in this setting. He would lean on the counter, insides of his wrists pointing out at me, hands pointing back at himself, and survey me coolly and silently. Unconvinced.

Upstairs was the classical section; you went up there if you felt like looking smart.

20. MJ FEET

North of the bookstore, a Santa Fe–looking stuccoed place to buy Birkenstocks and ponchos. A hangout for preppy bohemian girls, such as I was trying hard not to be. I wanted to be something more difficult, something other than what I was. I held a very deep misunderstanding about the world. I had this idea that if I wanted to be among people who were different from me, I should disguise my true self and become more like them. I perceived other people to be more authentic than me, and so in order to be more authentic, I became less what I was in the first place. I counterfeited in order to feel real or, more accurately, in order to hang around what seemed realer than the thing I started out as. You could call it class drag. But that was what the Ave was *for,* for some of us.

21. THE SOAP BOX

Oh the Soap Box, where I used to buy rain-scented talcum to sprinkle in my armpits so boys would love me.

22. BUS STOP AT FORTY-FIFTH AND THE AVE

You waited and looked in the window of Pier 1 Imports. Maybe you bought drugs while you waited. Maybe you went inside Pier 1 and bought instead violet pastilles, which were *from France.* Then you caught the 30 back to Laurelhurst, or the 7 up to Broadway, which was even cooler than the Ave, or the 43, which went everywhere and took forever to get there. I still have dreams where I am trapped on the 43.

23. THE NEPTUNE

The Neptune was the cavernous old repertory cinema just off the Ave at the corner of Brooklyn and Forty-fifth in the University District. The Neptune movie calendar went up on your refrigerator if you had cool parents, or on your bedroom wall if you were fending for yourself, coolness-wise. In my case both. The two-tone calendar was always heavily magneted to the refrigerator; it needed to be restrained because the light stuff of the newsprint flapped so easily in the slightest breeze, for instance, when you opened the fridge door. In my room the calendar was thumbtacked in a place of honor on the corkboard over the old armchair where I liked to read.

In tenth grade I made a new best friend, a boy who was two years older than me. Chris was a punk kid, with a shock of dyed-white hair, pegged black jeans, a motorcycle jacket, and a penchant for wearing pajama shirts by day. (Eventually he would go on to form the band the Presidents of the United States of America with my brother.) We went to the same school; he had been there all along, like an orchid growing on a tree you've looked at a thousand times. When it came to movies, we went to *everything*. The double feature of *Metropolis* and *Eraserhead* made me want to die, but I sat through the whole thing anyway.

Chris and I both had our own kinds of love trouble; I for one liked to go into dark and dangerous places with strangers or near-strangers and let them touch me. But in the Neptune, all that fell away. I was with my friend, who was a boy, and who, I somehow knew, would never touch me like that. Sometimes we would pretend to mash, with our hands over each other's mouths so we weren't really kissing. This ironic playacting at being teens making out at the movies was indescribably hilarious to us. We'd already been in so much trouble that there was an illicit thrill in pretended innocence.

24. THE SCIENTOLOGISTS

They stood on the same corner for years and asked you, every time, "Are you curious about yourself?" If you were, they took you upstairs and quizzed you until you were too hungry to sit there any longer. At least that was the report from the one person I ever knew who was curious about himself.

25. THE CONTINENTAL

Known in our family simply as "The Greek." A perfect restaurant: linoleum and vinyl and hugging owners and a dusting of feta on all the food. Sometimes the giant windows were open to the street and the smelly sunshine poured in, but usually it was a place to hide from the rain, full of steaming wet coats and intense conversations. I went here with anyone and everyone, or with a book. One great day in 1986 I ate all three separate meals here.

26. URBAN RENEWAL

Unbelievably cool record store (mostly British imports, in lovely thick fresh plastic sleeves).

27. GRAND ILLUSION

A tiny cinema with a single coveted love seat toward the back of the theater, perfect for making out or just snuggling with your pals. The shabby attached coffee shop was a kind of gatehouse for the north Ave, which was sadder and emptier and dustier and dreamier than the south end. It was at the Grand Illusion I met my friends Susie and Greg, mods about town. They were pretty strict about following mod fashion. I knew many like them, girls and boys who clung fiercely to the aesthetic tenets of a certain alternative subculture—mod, rockabilly, punk—as a kind of bulwark against perhaps a chaotic home life and maybe as a way of regimenting existence itself. Cuff width, plaid scale, hair length—these things mattered because something has to, because nothing does. They downed mochas and roared off on their vintage Vespas and Lambrettas. Or took the bus, usually, because the scooters were always breaking down.

28. NORTH OF FIFTIETH

Here be dragons.

29. NELLY STALLION

Nelly Stallion was a small clothes shop, European and smart and sort of terrifying. Also, expensive. I can recall every item of clothing I ever bought there. The clothes were not black, not punk, not mod. In fact, they didn't seem to follow rules at all; they were eccentric and charming and somehow British-seeming. I bought a pair of plaid pants, a creamy bunchy sweater, a frock scattered with flowers. I treasured my Nelly Stallion buys for years; found them impossible to toss even when they'd grown threadbare. Nelly Stallion was like a portal—you stepped from the grimy street through its doors and you found yourself transported, Pevensie-like, to an outpost of the Great World.

30. CAFE ALLEGRO

You kind of . . . graduated . . . up to the Allegro. Where the Last Exit was cavernous and the Grand Illusion was an aerie, the Allegro was a narrow, tight space. The coffee was roasted so dark it gave you a stomachache; even with cream in it, it still tasted like you were drinking it black.

The Allegro bulletin board was just a couple square feet, propped above the pastry case with its inevitable mazurkas. It was the intelligence center of the whole Ave. You checked it every day. Maybe some boy had seen you and asked around about you and wanted to meet you. Maybe a friend was leaving town and had no way to reach you. Relationships hinged on the Allegro bulletin board.

Were the girls more beautiful at the Allegro? I don't know.

Maybe it was just that there were more girls who looked the way I wanted to look. There was Sarah, who sometimes modeled—she was the one all the boys wanted to fuck. There was Marg and her best friend, Chrissy, a matched set of famously beautiful best friends, one fair and one dark, both mods, both severely dressed, with anoraks and black sweaters and sideways haircuts.

And there was Jess. Jess worked behind the counter. She had longish flat 1970s hair that hung in a perfect curtain. She had a flat hard body and a flat hard face. How did this all add up to beauty? She was so mean, hard like her biceps. She was a total hippie—batik T-shirts, dangly earrings—but she was severe enough, mean enough, dirty enough to read as punk. "What?" she'd ask when you went up to order, as if she had no fucking clue why you might be standing there.

Her looks sugared the pill. Her looks were tautological: You wanted to look at her because she was so so good to look at. When you looked, what you saw was not a passive, diffident beauty but someone looking back, hard, a person on whom nothing was lost. Also, a person acting like a total bitch.

I knew all this because I went there and looked at her a lot. Pretending to read my book, I'd watch her, and she'd catch my eye and stare back unabashed. If I asked her to, say, refill the empty half-and-half pitcher, she'd look at me as if I were out of my fucking mind.

At what point then did she become my mother? Not that she knew she was my mother or behaved like my mother, not that she nurtured me in any way at all. She barely ever favored me with a word. But she always kept her eye sternly on me.

Jess herself seemed resolutely asexual, though I later learned of torrid affairs and complex intrigues. This quality of holding back was very important for me to see. She held herself apart a little. She didn't pretend she wasn't beautiful; there was nothing coy in her. But she wasn't very interested in using her beauty's power. That fascinated me. I had never thought of that as an option—just letting your beauty lie around, unused. She was a model of a different way of being.

But that didn't make her my mother. What made her my mother was the way she witnessed me. She supervised me. When I came in with one of the multitude of dopey guys I hung around with, her eyes would narrow. She would look at me, then at the boy or man in question, then back at me, all but semaphoring "Are you fucking kidding me? This one's even worse than the last!" And then she would give me a little half smile that suggested I had once again fulfilled all her worst suspicions. The bad news she gave me about myself—well, I didn't know what to do with it. But I got it. I got the news.

January 18, 1982, age fifteen

You know what Steve's mom and my mom decided? That we couldn't be in a house alone together! Isn't that ridiculous. It's like, let's not trust anybody and be proper and make sure everyone retains their purity even though it's none of our business.

11

Recidivist Slutty Tendencies in the Pre-AIDS-Era Adolescent Female

A Case Study

AUTHORS Written by the adolescent female under consideration, some thirty years later. No other author has a meaningful intellectual stake in the writing of this article, though many individuals gave technical assistance.

KEY TERMS Adolescence, sexuality, sleeping bag, experimentation, child of divorce, impaired judgment, mental health, Volvo backseat, self-esteem, despair.

ABSTRACT This paper attempts to ascertain the causes of the near-rabbit levels of sexual activity in the subject, one adolescent female; the activity in question took place between the years 1980 and 1985. Certain things have come up in the subject's life that are making the subject curious—sexual feelings, teen feelings have come surging back and the subject would like to know why this is happening and why it happened in the first place. The paper's findings are inconclusive.

. . .

INTRODUCTION The female adolescent we studied demonstrated a compulsive need to attract, maintain, and indulge male sexual attention. There is some confusion as to when the condition began. Male sexual attention seemed always to be present in the subject's life, beginning at approximately age twelve. The child at this age was still a little chunky and had a giant puff of brown hair and often carried a book around with her, almost like a small-scale shield. It's apparent that at first the attention was unwelcome, at times visited upon the child with a certain amount of urgency and intimacy. When the subject was fourteen, late in the year of 1980, she began to pursue male attention, like the cartoon cat who turns around and begins to chase the dog. From there on out, her pursuit was dedicated; the subject was never without a boyfriend or several. She seemed to need to stack them, like cordwood for winter. Sexual activity was ongoing, occasionally fervent, but usually desultory or mechanical or dutiful. What this study is attempting to ascertain is *why*. Why did she do this?

CASE PRESENTATION Let us proceed to the subject's history, touching again on the problem of onset. When the subject was approximately five, her father moved out of the family home and a friendly hairy hippie moved in. The hippie brought with him a new circle of acquaintanceship, mostly very jolly. In the summers, the subject's impromptu, patchwork family lived in a cabin on a northern island in Washington State. The girl liked to sleep outside on the straw-colored, sweet-smelling grass. This was especially good in August, when the Perseid fell through the sky like a thousand fainting maidens and the subject could watch them falling as she drifted off to sleep. The girl, now approximately thirteen, lay just so, watching the Perseid, when one of the jolly friends emerged from the cabin and climbed into her sleeping bag. She felt his long hard thighs and then here came his CROTCH in his cutoffs—she felt all that against her soft thighs and her underpants with the sprung elastic. She stared straight up at the sky as if nothing were happening. She lay still as can be, but even so, she felt what she didn't want to feel, inside his cutoffs: what scholars can only surmise was her first erect penis. The subject then heard her mother's voice call from the porch: "Claire! Good night!" The sound of her mother's voice sent the hippie out of her sleeping bag and away through the night. The girl didn't think to tell her mother what had happened. She climbed out of the now-repulsive bag, a confinement, and thought, What have I done? Because while she undeniably had a terrible stomachache, some part of her had liked the attention.

At fourteen she acquired her first boyfriend. He was a cross-country phenom, a marathoner at age sixteen, with a barrel chest and long legs and floppy Steve Prefontaine hair. With this genial partner the girl had her first experience of oral sex, in her boyfriend's stick-shift Honda in the parking lot of the University of Washington Arboretum, the great, dangerous, crime-ridden, bosky sward that lay between her house and his. By "oral sex," of course we refer to fellatio, not cunnilingus, which was entirely out of the question. He didn't ask for it; the subject took his penis into her mouth of her own initiative. He came almost immediately and she tasted for the first time semen's grapefruity tang. He bought her a chocolate shake from Dick's Drive-In afterward. A treat. In return, aside from the shake, he inserted his fingers into the girl's vagina and thrust them there over and over, which didn't really feel that great. But the subject liked having a boyfriend, and the thought that a girlfriend might not perform sexual favors never occurred to her. Sometimes the boyfriend's eyes lost all focus and seemed to become almost black in color. When this happened, it was plain to the girl that the sexual attentions she was visiting upon him were taking over his whole being, making some regions of him go dark and other regions light up. This made her feel all-powerful, like Gigantor. Nonetheless, it seemed a little unfair that he should get to be transported in this manner, but she did not. Maybe the feeling of being transported would overtake her when they Did It. She knew they were going to because the boyfriend had been carrying a condom in his red Gore-Tex wallet for at least a month. She felt its ring-shaped bump in an inner pocket when she fished out dollars for hamburgers.

The feeling of being transported did *not* overtake her when they Did It, an event that occurred in the boyfriend's basement bedroom. First the pair attempted It in the back of his father's Scout, which didn't take. The car was parked on a hill and the two would-be fornicators kept rolling apart. Consummation was achieved instead in the boyfriend's bed, with Led Zep on the turntable. He had bought a sixer from his neighborhood corner store, a known source. He was one of those tall, confident kids who never had a problem buying beer, part of what made him a desirable boyfriend. The girl and the boy sat on the edge of his bed and drank one, passing it silently back and forth. "Kashmir" thundered away. Maybe it wasn't such a hot idea to introduce so much bombast to a mutual deflowering? The boy leaned over and turned off the lights. This, along with "Kashmir," seems like a piece of mismanagement in retrospect. Anyway. They took their clothes off. The subject lay back. There was no question: He would be on top. They kissed for a while, naked. No one giggled. This was serious. The entry was blunt force non-trauma, that is, it felt too big for the receptacle but otherwise basically uninteresting.

At first it was boys the same age as the subject, or only a bit older. The boys were brainy classmates from her progressive prep school, with Guatemalan spreads on their beds and climbing gear stashed in their closets and calculus textbooks on their neat desks. By the time the girl was sixteen, though, she had branched out. Her school was small, and she'd run through anyone of interest. It was easy to be picked up by men in coffeehouses—almost as if they were there waiting to be picked up by a teenage girl, which would have been terribly wicked of them. Though the subject was experienced beyond her years, she was too innocent to believe that wickedness like that could exist—though it was in fact exactly what was happening to her. The subject loved the power she held over the men. She loved the Moment: when the grown-up would turn to kiss her for the first time, and his eyes would go soft with lust, and she wouldn't be feeling lust in return, just as she hadn't with her first boyfriend. But now that emotional inequity felt like power, felt like control: to make a grown man go soft (and also: hard) like that! It made her feel kind of crazy with power. She saw it as a specific power unto herself, and didn't or wouldn't see that any ardent young girl would've sufficed. (There should be a specific name for this fallacy, the fallacy where you fit another person's sexual proclivities very well, and feel that it's because of some quality inherent solely in you, when of course it could easily be satisfied by anyone of vaguely similar shape and form. And age.)

An aside on the question of pleasure: The subject didn't really get much pleasure from all this fornicating she was doing. The compulsion wasn't to feel good, it was to enjoy the feeling of making someone want her, of making someone else feel good.

Frequency of condition was high, in fact constant.

Relieving factors were seemingly nonexistent; that is, the subject never stopped, she was like a shark. Occasionally the subject liked hanging out with her girlfriends—for instance drinking tea and talking about metaphysics with Talia on the massive green velvet couch in the living room of Talia's father, who was a neurosurgeon and owned a Morris Louis painting that hung, rainbow-hued yet somehow sad, over the fireplace. On the opposite wall was a piece of yarn art so exuberantly frayed that it possessed an almost diarrhea-like explosiveness, a piece of art that for whatever reason the subject loved to contemplate. But then night fell and it was time to go off somewhere with some boy and she always did, leaving Talia there with the tea and the ideas and the art.

Aggravating factors were also nonexistent or maybe they were constant, hard to tell which—at any rate unchanging.

Other health history is ambiguous. The subject appeared to be in good mental health, though this might have been a function of her naturally cheerful—in fact annoyingly milkmaidish—face. Truth be told, she was miserable but didn't know how to say it, or even think it. She sought no treatment for her misery, aside from the constant fucking and boyfriend-acquiring, which was more killing than curing. Also, the drugs, which are not the purview of this study but whose effects cannot be denied or gainsaid.

As for family history, the subject's maternal grandmother was the first woman to be divorced in her North Seattle parish. It's true that she didn't *want* to be a divorced woman—her husband left her without so much as a by-your-leave. Nonetheless a divorced woman, intentionally or not, she was. It was a scandalous thing to be in that time and that place, and she augmented the reputation by spending several decades as a very drunken cocktail waitress at the Lake City Elks club. The subject's mother, as we touched upon earlier, dumped the subject's father for a hippie eight years her junior. Does that make the subject's mother a slut? Hardly. But it represents some kind of antecedent.

The condition was terminated by context. That is, the compulsive sex continued well on into her twenties, but of course once she went to college, her high level of sexual desire no longer seemed like an outlier kind of compulsion, or so she fondly believed. At college everyone just fucked and fucked, and the perverse thing was to abstain. So finally she was normal, and therefore her condition was no longer a condition. Except years later, in her forties, it was again, and maybe it never had gone away? Must one fuck all the time in order to be oversexed? Or could it just be a dormant quality?

DATA ANALYSIS Whatever your opinion of frequent sexual congress, let us assume for the purpose of this study that consensual sex should provide an increase in personal happiness, which was a widely held belief during the era we are discussing. Represented below is a visual expression of the data we compiled regarding the subject's sexual activity.

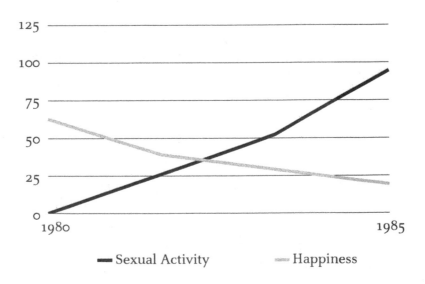

. . .

UNDERLYING CAUSES The adolescent was affected by factors historical, cultural, familial, psychological, and possibly mythological.

Historically, this was an era when forces combined to create an excess of sexual freedom. Birth control was readily available, norms were tolerant, and there was little sense of sex being something that had repercussions, aside from pregnancy, which was for morons. In other words, it was that tiny two-decade window between 1963, Philip Larkin's famous start date for sexual intercourse, and the mid-1980s, when AIDS began to make itself known. Sex, for that short while, seemed a mostly benign thing, possibly even an improving hobby, like learning the dulcimer or making your own yogurt.

Culturally, the subject's adolescence occurred during a time when kids roamed the countryside and city streets unsupervised; a time when sex had been let off its leash and was loose in the world. There was a sort of tangerine-colored ferment in the air. And it applied to little girls as much as it did to grown-ups—maybe even more.

From the time the subject was eleven or twelve, she could hardly go anywhere without some man or boy talking to her in a vaguely predatory way. And it was not as if she was done up in short shorts. She wore painter's pants, smocks, old T-shirts. But there was something afoot that made her a perfectly acceptable object of widespread on-the-street lust. On the bus, on the sidewalks, men talked to her constantly. The banality of their language struck her even at the time, the multiple variations that could be found on "hey" and "girl" and "smile." The subject remembers being seen—the opposite of invisible: ultra-visible—before she was ready to be looked at.

She wasn't the only one. The gaze of that era was turned

resolutely toward little girls: Brooke Shields as a twelve-year-old prostitute in *Pretty Baby;* Jodie Foster, *Taxi Driver,* same deal; on the cover of Led Zeppelin's *Houses of the Holy,* naked young girls crawled up a stony hill that looked like it would be hard on their knees. The Foreigner album cover *Head Games* showed fourteen-year-old Lisanne Falk looking sexily terrified, cowering in fear near a urinal. The elites were far from immune: Mariel Hemingway snuggled in bed with Woody Allen, eating Chinese food and watching old movies, curving her pillowy beautiful seventeen-year-old lips into a smile, as if this were the most fun thing ever. And of course the Altamont of the 1970s of little girls: Roman Polanski's statutory rape of thirteen-year-old Samantha Gailey.

The sexual revolution appeared to be really great for everyone. (Until AIDS.) Who's not in favor of sex? Only retrograde fools are against sex. The sexual revolution appeared to be a victimless revolution. Except it sort of . . . wasn't. Once sex was set free, it ran like a fire and consumed everything in its path, especially girls. Girls found themselves in a new landscape. In this landscape, girls wandered without parental supervision much of the time; and girls were acceptable objects of desire. This study doesn't need to provide a chart to explain what happened next. You do the fucking math.

The subject's familial role as a younger sister may be a factor. The girl wanted to be just like her big brother. She wanted to be a boy; short of that, she wanted to be as close to boys as possible. She utterly rejected the notion she was essentially a girl—worse, a pre-woman. When she turned fifteen, when she truly could no longer deny she was a girl, she developed a new strategy. She wouldn't be a boy, but she would be as *near to boys* as she could possibly be. Them inside of her seemed like just about the right proximity. This study sort of wishes that the subject could've done like the protagonist of Virginia Woolf's

Orlando, a nobleman who woke one day to find himself trans-
formed into a woman: "He stood upright in complete nakedness
before us, and while the trumpets pealed Truth! Truth! Truth!
we have no choice left but confess—he was a woman." If only
Woolf could've worked such magic on our subject, and rendered
her transformation from boy to woman as easy, as *triumphant*
as Orlando's.

As for the psychological explanation, well, this study thinks
psychology is sort of bullshit, but here goes: The subject as a
child had a strong desire to reunite her parents, an objective that
could, she felt, be achieved only by being as sunny and cheerful
and compliant as possible. Her angers and resentments went
underground, as it were, remaining hidden and suppressed
until they eventually mushroomed into this weird sexual free-
fall. Too, the mother had sexualized the home environment by
introducing into it her lover, or lovah if you will. The daughter
was perhaps unconsciously mimicking the mother's strategy. In
any case, sleeping with men, especially with older men, was a
way to lure her father back home, and also a way to return to
and take control of the thing with the sleeping bag. I mean,
the study is pretty sure that's how a therapist might see it. In
fact, a therapist weighed in that one time: He said the departure
of her father from the family home made her a ripe candidate
for "hypersexuality." When the therapist said this, the subject
looked at him and started cracking up. Hypersexuality! "Is that
a nice way of calling me a slut?" the subject asked. The therapist
paused with a comic's impeccable timing. "Yes, yes, it is," he said
in his rueful way.

All of these factors contributed to the subject's sluttiness.
But this study feels the most useful explanation, perhaps, is
mythological. A mythology of sex itself. The subject infused the
act of sex with unconscious mystical power. Why did she put
that power into sex and nothing else? She wanted sex to achieve

something for her, something outside of itself. This something could have a name: connection, redemption, purpose, pleasure, pure feeling. But really what she wanted was for sex to make her known. You have edges, you are something, you are here, you exist, defined by these hands, this mouth, this penis. Sex was supposed to do all that. It didn't.

The study is disappointing. It attempted to determine why, and while it found a handful of really good answers, what has emerged is the larger mystery of sex itself. The author of the study wasn't in the mood for larger mysteries. The author of the study is just feeling really, really confused and trying to make sense of things.

August 6, 1985, age eighteen

I wonder if we are destined never to be in love
with anyone because we're TOO romantic?

12

Jump Cuts

The Seven Gables Theatre is arranged over three floors, each maroon-er than the last. There are maroon drapes absolutely everywhere, including a heavy, labial pair hanging at the entrance to the theater itself. Maroon-and-gold-and-black-patterned carpeting covers the first and second floors. Dusty, stiff, maroon-upholstered furniture clogs both lobbies. In the theater itself the seats are maroon velvet, the color of dried blood.

But the theater of course is not where we work, except to clean up empty Junior Mints boxes and spilled popcorn after screenings. There's nothing to *do* in the theater, and this is after all our place of work.

We wear narrow black skirts and plain white shirts. We smooth our hair into bobs or tight ponytails. Ours is an aesthetic of refusal. We are mods. We plunder thrift shops trying to find clothes that are plain enough. It's the middle of the '80s and nothing is plain enough. We are pretty committed to being as pretentious as humanly possible. However, in this benighted pre-Internet era, it's hard to know what exactly to pretend to. We know one thing for sure: Europe is good. So we love our jobs at the art-house cinema, which rarely shows an American film.

The box office is a spacious room, always occupied by Grant and Kristen. Grant, our manager, is a just-handsome, juicy-lipped, slightly bug-eyed gay man—boy, really—only a couple of years older than us. We have never had a gay friend before, or not that we knew of anyway. Grant is out, proud, and above all loud. Kristen is Grant's familiar, her witchy laughing head next to his all the time. Grant and Kristen are the theater mom and dad; we are their flock.

We complain about going to work, but really we like it. We like having a uniform and a paycheck and a clear set of tasks. We have active love lives, but our love lives aren't as lovely as life at the Seven Gables, a whole little world devoted to romance and art.

The lead-up to showtime quickens. Kristen imperiously ejects us all from the ticket booth, even though her change-making is notoriously sloppy, and we swarm the concession stand, keeping an eye out for cute boys. We have, it must be said, fans. Boys come to see grim Swedish dramas and obscure documentaries because of us. We are known for our style.

Working alongside us is none other than Eleanor Lund, of "*We* call them windies and *we* don't think they're funny" fame. The whole staff calls her "Windy." The reason everyone is so ready to mock her is that (a) we are all assholes and (b) she is as prissy as ever. She is still a pin-neat blonde, she still looks askance at bad behavior. (For heaven's sake, why is she working at an art-house movie theater, traditionally the first job of every pretentious high-school fuckup on earth?) She eyes us censoriously as we giggle and jostle; she wipes up after our Coke spills; she says "Thank you!" to every customer.

We take a package of Manner wafers from the case and throw it on the floor. The Seven Gables sells Manner wafers because they are European. "Oops!" we say. "Broken!" We put the cookies in the back room to eat later and get back to the business of scooping and selling.

But hush now, the previews are over and the film is starting. We pour some coffee and push through the maroon curtains into the theater.

Helena Bonham Carter's head is astonishing. It's massive, yet adorable. It seems to bobble on the stem of her neck. Atop that giant head is a big pile of hair and then, incredibly, there's a hat riding the whole thing. The head looks like it might just tumble off and roll away. HBC, in the immortal, career-making role of Lucy Honeychurch (after whom my own child will be named many years later), is gazing petulantly over the rooftops of Florence, which is what she's going to be doing for a while. We know this because we've been showing *A Room with a View* for more than a month and at this point we've seen it countless times. Every night is a summer afternoon in that theater.

HBC and Maggie Smith, as her guardian, begin to bicker about the view. It's funny because the view is so sublime and their discussion of it so petty. We slink down in our seats, watching as the two lady travelers explore the pension and join the other Brits, including George (played by the unbelievably hot Julian Sands) and his earnest father, for an awkward supper. HBC glowers and pouts the while.

We'll go back to work just after Miss Catharine puts the cornflowers in her hair. This is one of our favorite moments in the movie, when the octogenarian gentlewoman Miss C is given piles of cornflowers by George and his kind-eyed father, who says, "There are no jewels more becoming a lady. I like to see them in your hair." And so father and son delicately, carefully poke cornflowers into Miss Catharine's gray halo, and she looks crazy and girlish and romantic and happy all at once. The corn-flowers glow almost electric blue in the shimmering Florentine light of her hotel room; her grin hovers Cheshirely, in love with the idea of love. It's a strangely thrilling sight. We love Miss Catharine; she's so much more fun than Lucy Honeychurch.

We go back to the concession stand to make some popcorn for the stragglers who mysteriously buy their snacks once the movie is under way. We will never understand this habit—didn't you *come here* to forget about hunger, about time, about everything? At any rate we love making popcorn; it seems a godlike task. The swirl of thick yellow oil; the scoop of seeds, and then it comes, the smell, the sweet burning greasy yellow smell. Is there another smell so instantly evocative of nothing but its own self, another smell so *famous*?

We watch the popcorn pop while Windy—oops, Eleanor—cleans the heads of the Coke machine and then we go lie down on one of the maroon couches, fatigued by our exertions. After a while we retrieve the Manner wafers from the back room and eat them, getting crumbs all over the couch.

We slip into the theater just in the nick of time, as Lucy wades through the barley and poppies toward George. She looks as peevish as ever. We prefer our heroines more tomboyish, like Jo March or Elizabeth Bennet. Lucy Honeychurch seems like a boring girlie girl. Nonetheless, this: George plows through the barley toward her and everything is blond, blond, blond: his hair, the field, the sunlight, the hills. He grabs her gigantic bob-bly pompadoured head and kisses her, openmouthed, bending her back. A good old sexy movie kiss, except in this film, in this milieu of repression, it's revolutionary. That's what we want, a revolutionary kiss. That's what we've been looking for. A kiss that will be an agent of change; a kiss after which nothing can be the same.

Lucy's into it too—she doesn't pull away until Maggie Smith calls her name. She startles a little, and we see her beautiful moony face, and it's not just that her lips look bruised, her whole self does. We are filled with yearning as we watch. (Could there ever be an incursion as absolute for us, fallen girls who'd lost our virginities back in the early '80s? As absolute as George's sun-drenched tonguing of Lucy, the sun as much an intruder as the tongue? There is something in us still that yearns to be corrupted in that exact way.)

We slip back out and clean the concession area in a brief frenzy, carpet-sweeping and Dust Buster–ing and straightening. It won't do to have popcorn littering the floor for the nine o'clock showing.

As we work, Grant comes dancing through the concession area, thrusting his hips and singing "Relax," hitting the word "come" hard. Kristen leans against the doorjamb, arms crossed, laughing. Grant goes dancing every night after work and brings new moves back to us, showing us the latest outrageously unstoppered, aqueous shimmy he's picked up, sliding hips-first across the carpet. His brash, joyous thrusting is new to us, and sort of wonderful. We gather around him, black-and-white birds, with our dreams of Europe and of being kissed, really kissed. And our suspicion that because we are bad we can never receive such a kiss. Kisses like that are for girls who are good. Years later, decades later, some of us—Natalie, Susie, Martha, Kristen, Claire—will still want to be kissed just like that. Decades later, when we are middle-aged ladies, we will be susceptible to incursions, to people who make us feel like something is *happening to us.*

. . .

Grant, grinning naughtily, leads us back into the theater. He's got a little bag of popcorn that he shares. It's time for our favorite part, maybe everyone's favorite part, if only they'd admit it: Mr. Beebe and the beautiful George Emerson and Lucy's delicious hilarious younger brother, Freddy, all go swimming. They arrive at the pond in jaunty single file, whereupon George and Freddy strip naked, proudly full-frontal and totally gorgeous. Mr. Beebe can't resist—it's never quite clear if his glee is or isn't lecherous—and jumps in too. Mr. Beebe is our stand-in; we too want to join in, want to be boys with them. We want to be acting wild, acting silly, in the beautiful green pond with the beautiful naked boys. The very light is verdant and cozy and English and somehow comic; the opposite of all that high-minded Italian yellow sunshine. Grant sighs and passes the popcorn. We munch and gaze. The rest of the audience is laughing, with almost a note of hysteria. It's because of the penises, they make everyone feel a little nervous. The scene's flouting of cinematic convention makes a kind of echo of the characters' flouting of social convention. But we don't laugh, we dream, yearning to be among boys.

Grant is after all our manager, and as soon as the scene is over, he shoos us out: Back to work. Back to the lobby. Leave behind the dream of love, the beautiful men, the primacy of romance and sex, the summer afternoon.

But what about Eleanor "Windy" Lund, the pariah of this story? She's just a digression, interesting only in the sense that she is and always has been the antonym of everything we want to be: first tomboys, then bad girls. When we come out of the theater she, of course, is diligently doing her job behind the counter;

in the absence of customers, she wipes the surfaces down with a rag. The air is greasy and almost viscous with the smell of popcorn.

Now a patron pushes through the maroon curtains. We lie down on the couch and watch as Eleanor serves him. She is poised and quiet and unsmiling as she takes his money, gives him his change. Her hair hangs in a shining curtain.

In that moment, something about Eleanor Lund passes through the tough membrane of our disdain. Or maybe something chemical and glandular kicks in upstairs in the teen medulla. Whatever has happened, Eleanor Lund suddenly looks different.

She is slow, and un-daring, and uptight. She is maybe a little boring. She doesn't need to prove anything; she is exactly what she is through and through. We look at her there in the yellow light of the popcorn machine. She seems entirely unfamiliar to us—even exotic. Beautiful. Maybe something will happen to her, and she will be illuminated by love.

May 1986, age nineteen

Everyone's a critic here,
and the critics are always,
always winning.

13

A Is for Acid:
An Oberlin Abecedarium

A Is for Acid

Acid was what we did. Like homework. We did it all the time, starting our very first week of our freshman year. We did it even though we weren't even sure we really liked it. "Leave me alone you crazy tripsters," wrote my roommate Fred in an admonishing open letter to acidheads everywhere, untroubled by the fact that he himself was high on acid as he wrote it. And yes, my roommate was a boy. I had a boy roommate because (a) I didn't really know how to be friends with girls and (b) it was *Oberlin*.

The thing about acid was its portability. Also, its non-injectedness. You didn't even have to snort it. We were against snorting things. Snorting was yuppie. Acid held no such bourgeois associations (or so we thought), and yet unlike heroin, it posed no needlesome threats. It was *paper*, for Pete's sake. No biggie. We spent our lives surrounded by paper: books, notebooks, drawing pads, etc. A little more paper wasn't going to hurt us.

Aside from taking drugs, Fred and I had other shared interests, like . . . well, I can't think of any right this minute. Fixing complicated midnight snacks in our vegetarian dorm's smelly kitchen? Giggling? Trying to make our handwriting quirkier? (In the days before social media, quirky handwriting was one of the only ways you could demonstrate to the world how interesting you were.) All that fall of 1985 we took acid with our pal Elizabeth. We would roam the town all night long, going to parties or just drifting around dampening our feet in the early snow, and then go back to our room and still have a few hours of high left. These hours were mostly spent listening to Echo and the Bunnymen. When I met Fred, he liked to pair acid with Pink Floyd, which he saw as a classic gesture and I saw as a pathetic failure of imagination.

While the dark music played, I would gaze at the copy of *On the Banks of Plum Creek* by Laura Ingalls Wilder, which I'd brought from home. The soft lines of Garth Williams's illustrations made a kind of pillowy landing as you came down from your trip. I spent a lot of time thinking about how impressive the sunbonnet was, as a technology.

B Is for Butt Rock

The tavern in town was the Tap House and the drinking age was eighteen—hey, that was *my* age! The Tap House, a long shadowy wooden room, looked like any tavern you've ever been in. It was drearily, delightfully exemplary. There, with Fred and Elizabeth, I drank watery pitchers of Rolling Rock, which at the time was a strictly regional beer and had a Rust Belt exoticism. I played pinball and got good. But what I did most of all was put quarters in the jukebox. We were the kind of kids who'd cycled through everything by the time we got to college. We loved the obscure, the difficult, the hard to find. A painfully skinny girl who wore great wings of black eyeliner had a radio show on WOBC, the

Oberlin station, which she called *The Difficult Listening Hour*, and I found that just unbelievably, spectacularly cool.

But at the Tap House things were different. Simpler. Much has been made of the '90s as the era of irony. If so, my '90s began in 1985, when I walked into the Tap House in my ripped black tights and my old-man shoes, strode across the wide unvarnished planks, put a quarter in the jukebox, and punched in the number for "Cum On Feel the Noize." You got two choices for a quarter, and my second choice was always, always AC/DC's "You Shook Me All Night Long." The German philosopher Friedrich von Schlegel said that irony is the simultaneous giving and taking back of a thing. I hadn't read Schlegel yet, but I was performing perfect Schlegelian irony as I whacked the pinball machine and sang along at the top of my lungs: "KNOCKING ME OUT WITH THOSE AMERICAN THIGHS." College, I was quickly finding out, made me feel trapped and anxious, and I sort of hated it there, and butt rock was like a little valve.

C Is for Chlamydia

Flash forward to the summer of 1986: I'm home in Seattle. I go to see my beloved doctor for a routine checkup. He flips open my file and I see, written in big purple letters, the word CHLAMYDIA. All caps. I don't remember having been tested for chlamydia or even discussing it with him, ever. I ask, "Why does that piece of paper say chlamydia?" He responds without missing a beat, "Oh, that's what we call you around the office."

I didn't have it, as it turned out. But not for lack of trying.

A Is for Acid: An Oberlin Abecedarium

D Is for David

My brother David, whom I worshipped, came to visit me at Oberlin.

My hero-slash-brother and I ate lunch and then went out to the quad and sat down on a bench—I mean to say, what? Who even *sits* on benches? Had I ever sat on a bench before? Anyway, we did, we sat on a bench, and were we ever sorry we did, because someone had scrawled on that very bench: "FOR A GOOD TIME CALL CLAIRE DEDERER," and then my campus phone number. I turned red and looked guiltily at Dave, who seemed horrified yet unsurprised. I wondered who wrote it. There had been, there were, a lot of them. Derek, a frustrated post-disco tussle, which came to a mortifyingly quick ending; Graham, a blow job under shrubbery; Paul, an afternoon in my empty room; and more. More. More was my watchword. More was how I was navigating Oberlin.

My brother went into the dorm, and somehow acquired a rag, and tried to scrub it off. We never spoke of it again.

E Is for Ecstasy

I took it with two boys, best friends, both of whom had enormous heads and were the biggest hippies at Oberlin—that is, possibly the biggest hippies in the entire world. The three of us hugged euphorically, desperately, all night long, in my closet of all places. The hugging was *epic.* We emerged in the morning exhausted and filled with a vast sadness, as brown and flat as an Ohio cornfield in wintertime. For the following month I was more depressed than ever. The two big-headed hippies took up daily Buddhist meditation just to recover from the whole ordeal.

F Is for Feminism

Feminism was the most important ism. I wrote my friend Trish back in Seattle about them all—feminism, vegetarianism, existentialism—and told her about a Halloween party where you were supposed to go as your favorite ism. She wrote back: "You should go as jism!" But her letter came too late.

Feminism, for me, was an ethical theory of why I should like girls. Girls were fine, but for me they paled next to the glory that was boys. You know the old saying about Cary Grant: Women wanted him, men wanted to be him. That pretty much describes how I felt about *all boys.*

This was the feminism of my childhood. As a tomboy, I was, in my mind, by definition a libber. Feminism's lesson—that boys and girls are equal, so sweetly hammered into us by *Free to Be ... You and Me*—was translated by me to mean that girls could and should be more like boys.

At Oberlin, feminism wanted me actually to like girls. More than like them. It wanted me to imbue them with power. At Oberlin, the big men on campus were women. At the top of the heap were maybe five seriously famous lesbians. They were at least as charismatic as my brother. They moved across campus trailing a wake of envious, admiring susurration behind them. They weren't how I'd imagined lesbians would be. They had long hair. They invented glorious new ways of wearing clothes, often involving undershirts. The second week of school, one of them—it was blond-haired, petite Rebecca—petted my thigh as if it were a cat. The thigh in question was very hairy—I'm a hirsute creature if left unchecked. Absently, dreamily, Rebecca said, "Maybe you should consider shaving." I knew enough already to feel complimented. Feminism; the touch of a girl's hand. These things both suddenly seemed more interesting.

A Is for Acid: An Oberlin Abecedarium

G Is for Goddess

We stood in the dusky basement cafeteria at Harkness, the vegetarian cooperative where I lived. It smelled of cleaning fluid and
incense and the inevitable brewers' yeast. Maybe a just hint of
Dr. Bronner's soap. A wild-haired, zaftig, rosy-cheeked girl took
me by the hand and said, "I want you to meet someone." She led
me over to another wild-haired, zaftig, rosy-cheeked girl. Joining
our hands together she said, "Goddess, meet Goddess."

H Is for Hand

Having a roommate was hard on a chronic masturbator such
as myself. I had learned how to masturbate in the winter of
1983, when I was sixteen. Kinda late in the game considering I'd
been having sex for almost two years. At sixteen, I finally had
a boyfriend who knew about my clitoris—the very existence
of which had been up to that point entirely unknown to me.
He had clever fingers and stick-to-itiveness. Once he'd made me
come, it was all I wanted to do. I haunted his house, down the
street from my own. I learned his mother's work schedule so I
could pounce while she was away. I became utterly dependent
on him, though I didn't love him. I was interested in his digits. And then, one night, a month or so after my first orgasm
with him, I was lying on the couch at my dad's houseboat reading *Even Cowgirls Get the Blues*. Which is a really dirty book! I
started to get that feeling, and I slipped my hand into my underpants, and discovered that I could do it just as well as my boyfriend. I broke up with him the next day.

Once I figured out how to do it, I couldn't understand why
people didn't spend all their time masturbating. Good old right
hand, always there for me. Now, in my cinder-block-walled dorm

room, lying on my dorm bed, I tried hard not to, but . . . oh well. At last I thought I heard Fred's breathing slow and I stuck my paw in my holey underpants. Home.

I Is for Indignation, Righteous

I quit eating meat my first week at Oberlin, and at Christmas break went back to Seattle a proud and vocal vegetarian. I hoped my mother would try to serve me Jell-O, so I could explain it was made from cows' hooves and refuse it on account of my vegetarianism. She had never served me Jell-O before and didn't now. I also hoped someone would ask me if I was a lacto-ovo vegetarian, so I could answer, "I am a *moral* vegetarian." Sometimes they did ask, and answering gave me great satisfaction.

J Is for the Jesus and Mary Chain

I remember the winter of 1986 as essentially black and white. Lots of snow, lots of overcoats. I was starting to get really sick of this fucking cornfield and would go into Cleveland at the drop of a hat. I knew a little gang of punk-rock boys—well, "knew" is a strong word; I'd made out with one of them and liked the looks of the rest—who somehow had access to a station wagon. They were going into Cleveland to see the Jesus and Mary Chain and they let me come too, and as we filed into the dimly lit theater I thought I'd about die of happiness. There it was, good old life, happening all around me: the boring opening bands, the rocker girls and their gigantic hair, the ambient smell of beer, and best of all the strangers, everywhere you looked were strangers. Things were happening in the Cleve. The scene was crushingly, heartbreakingly rich and weird and full of possibility. I wanted to stay. I didn't want to go back to school. That's how much I hated Oberlin; it was making Cleveland look good. *Cleveland.*

For many years I wondered why I was so sad at Oberlin. Did I feel outclassed by it? Was I experiencing existential angst? Was I unfit for college life? Or maybe it was this: I missed rock shows and saltwater. I was a crabby complicated pretentious child. It was hard to admit the truth: I was homesick.

K Is for Key

I went out each night to the disco or the Rathskeller or the Tap House with my room key on a long string around my neck. No purse, no wallet, no money, no ID, no nothing. Just the key. I simply assumed—at college, and for years afterward—that everything else would be taken care of: admission to any bar, money, rides, food, drinks, everything, even the shelter the key unlocked. I'd take all that stuff, everything I was given, and never ever give back. Unless it suited me. And I didn't even realize I was doing it. I had no idea. I thought I was nice. If you'd asked me, I would've described myself as a nice person. The key bounced between my little breasts.

SPACE RESERVED: L Is Always for Love

Matthew was from a family of classical musicians and doctors, Ashkenazi Jews. Matthew had crow wings of black hair. Matthew knew about bands I'd never heard of and told jokes so dry that I didn't always know they were jokes. Matthew had rosy cheeks and dusky skin, like a heroine from *Ivanhoe*. Matthew's voice was throaty and was always saying the smartest thing. But I notice that I led with his Jewishness. His Jewishness was deeply moving and sexy to me, a kind of otherness that was absolute and impenetrable. I didn't know I was following a literary tradition in this feeling; in any case I wouldn't have liked it, wouldn't have liked the idea that I was one of Philip Roth's shiksas. My feeling of wanting to be Jewish, of wanting to be Matthew, was my secret, selfish animating force. Of course I couldn't become him: I was a big fair-haired Gentile Western girl, full of chatter and ardor and earnestness. The only possible solution was to fuck him.

M Is for Marriage

Fred looked at me ruefully as I pulled on my woolen overcoat and wrapped my big black scarf babushka-like around my head. "It's cozy here," he said, patting the bed. Not seductive, just friendly. We slept with our bunks pushed together, woke up in the morning asexually, unconsciously snuggled close. (He would come out the following fall.) I once struggled to the surface of sleep to find his finger in my nose. Now I turned my back on him and went out, down the long dorm hall, through the heavy front door, and into the swirling snow. I had to walk only as far as the North Quad, but I would've gone a lot farther. I would've used a clothesline tied to a building, as Laura Ingalls did in the blizzard.

I found the dorm, identified the correct yellow rectangle of light, and knocked on Matthew's window. He slid it open. He had, sort of, invited me over. "Oh, hey!" he said, looking surprised. I climbed in. I wanted him despite his reluctance, or probably because of it.

We kissed, more and more roughly, until he grabbed ahold of some of my belly fat and pinched it hard. "Oh," I said, hot and embarrassed. "Sorry." I was apologizing for the fat. "It doesn't matter," he said. "You're beautiful." I wasn't. You couldn't pinch beautiful, at least not in the waist. But I didn't care. *He* was beautiful. He was the most beautiful thing I had ever seen. I've since learned that—if you're lucky—you get to go to bed with maybe three or four people in your life who are so big and so brilliant and so perfect they blot out the sun. They *become* the sun. He was one of them, for me. Even though his bed was narrow and he was inexperienced. Even though he thought I was a chubster. Like he said, it didn't matter. You don't get to choose when or by whom you are going to be illuminated and maybe even eclipsed—deliciously, filthily eclipsed. It just happens and who knows why. Who even knows what to do about it, except fuck and fuck until the whole thing blows up.

We slid out of our clothes and kissed some more. He set my hands on my breasts and watched my fingers as they touched my nipples. The sheets were scratchy and hot. He came into me, for a while anyway, and then he was done. And then began the talking.

Matthew was planning something: our marriage. We would live in the suburbs. We would leave the house only at night. Our neighbors would wonder what we did all day long. "We'll be writing, and thinking, and listening to music," said Matthew. "We'll live on Kit Kats," he said. "We'll go out at night to buy them. That's all we'll eat. And we'll have a cat named Mr Whiskers II." Mr Whiskers was his cat back at home, whom he adored. We would take care of Mr Whiskers II and eat Kit Kats. We would listen to the Go-Betweens and read Raymond Carver. It was more than I could bear. I almost fainted from happiness—not because I thought it would ever happen but because he'd imagined it, and I was inside his imagination, a girl in a castle in the air.

In the morning I left before Matthew woke. I didn't want

to see the particular trapped look that would steal across his face when he rolled over and found me in his bed. I walked home through the bright, light gray snow to Fred, and we did the things real married people do: made coffee, nagged each other about our messy living quarters, told jokes to compensate for the terrible world.

N Is for Not Eating

Heartache and despair—these are normal feelings for the young, right? Then how come I found myself thinking about killing myself? How come I cried every day? How come, even as I pined for Matthew, I continued to compulsively fuck drunken friends and also enemies in bathrooms, on the quad, in my bed, behind the library?

And how come I quit eating?

I based my diet on some kind of Archie-comic-book idea of what girls eat to be thin: cottage cheese, grapefruit, black coffee. And it worked, too. Not eating hurt, or rather was uncomfortable, and therefore it focused all my attention on my body, I suppose in the way I wished Matthew would focus all his attention on my body. Maybe eating *a lot* would've achieved the same objective—that is, the objective of putting all the attention on my body. But not eating was a kind of hope—hope that I could make myself perfect enough for Matthew. Obsession requires at least a seed of hope. Obsession in fact is the same thing as baseless hope, and it's terrible.

Anyway, I wasn't hungry.

A Is for Acid: An Oberlin Abecedarium

O Is for Obsession

When I thought about Matthew, I felt an uncomfortable tingling in my forearms and hands. It was anxiety. I was anxious all the time, I had been anxious for years, but my anxiety now flowed into a single-pointed, sexualized focus. Everything would be okay if Matthew loved me. Everything would be okay if Matthew thought I was beautiful. Everything would be okay if I were as thin as I needed to be for Matthew to want me. Matthew filled my mind with thoughts. Well, "thoughts" is a strong word. When I say I was thinking about him, I don't mean thinking in the usual sense. I mean his face and name entered the stage of my brain like actors. My brain wasn't even as substantial as a stage. It was the merest proscenium, framing the starry, the glittering abstraction of Matthew's face and name. Ta-da.

P Is for Plastic Bags, and Privilege

Rushing to class I passed three especially rich, especially cool prep-school boys—the ones who had famous architects and art dealers for fathers. Each swung a plastic bag from his hand. They had taken to carrying their books in bags from the grocery store instead of in backpacks or the Danish schoolboy bags the kids from New York affected. The scope for the fine-tuning of slumming and reverse snobbery at Oberlin was infinite. I was as bad as anyone, with my ripped tights and my smelly thrift-store coats. The only people I knew at Oberlin who genuinely liked nice things were the people who had little money. My pal Elizabeth, for one, came from a working-class Italian family, and crowed openly when she got a new Perry Ellis scarf or a pair of Ray-Ban sunglasses.

Q Is for Quarry

Spring came, and it was the thing to go to the quarry, and jump off the ledge, and swim. I lay on a hot rock and watched all the swimming people. Matthew wasn't there. The quarry was for nude swimming, and Matthew was too punk for nudity. Everybody's bodies were so beautiful. I was glad I hadn't eaten for, like, five months. I covered my breasts with my arm, trying to look casual. My bottom got sunburned. The water was silky with some kind of exotic Ohioan mineral.

R Is for Roman Polanski

A mysterious, pale-skinned girl named Cassie appeared out of nowhere, midway through the year. She had been living in San Francisco, trying to make a film. She wore thrift-store turtle-necks and no bra and seemed to exist entirely in black-and-white. Which was perfect because she introduced the movies at the film-society screenings. Matthew and I went every week. If I expressed reluctance he'd call me a philistine and make me go anyway. We saw Polanski's *Knife in the Water*. It was terrifying, but I wasn't sure why. Every shot in the movie seemed to be about sex; in each scene, someone seemed like they were about to do sex or violence or both to someone else. It was the perfect movie to see with Matthew, whom I always felt was acting on me. My love for him made me feel truly helpless; I could not imagine getting over it. I felt hot and alive with him and sensed he'd prefer something a little less . . . well, just a little less.

Cassie was cool the way a corpse is cool; she was everything I, over-alive and ardent, was not. Maybe once a week I saw her at the front of the classroom the film society used as a kind of de facto art-house cinema. She leaned against the teacher's desk as she made her laconic opening remarks. It was hard not to look at her nipples, which stared back.

S Is for Saint Ann's

All the coolest girls had gone to Saint Ann's School in Brooklyn, an institution heretofore unknown to me. The Saint Ann's girls had smooth hair and equally flat affects. They always held a beer bottle when they danced, which should give you an idea of their exquisite self-containment, a quality I've never been accused of having. They wore perfectly plain black clothes, which were very difficult to find in those benighted days. They looked like the most expensive, chicest, most fuckable French schoolgirls you ever saw. Back in Brooklyn, they had slept with Beastie Boys when the Beastie Boys were still a punk band. They had famous parents. They inhabited an East Coast world I instinctively felt hostile toward, even as I obscurely coveted its acceptance, which was not forthcoming. The Saint Ann's girls didn't need anyone besides themselves. They ruled the school. When I left Oberlin I thought I was done with them forever, but it turned out they ruled all the schools. When I became a writer I discovered they edited all the newspapers and all the magazines. They wrote all the books. They went to all the parties. For the rest of my life, the Saint Ann's girls would be around, making me feel like a galumphing provincial.

T Is for Tour

Spring brought with it mud, melancholy, and midterms, but a select few bypassed the drear season altogether. Toward the end of the school year, it seemed like half of Oberlin packed up and left. They went on Tour. No need to explain or qualify or define. There was only one tour. The Deadheads seemed bound by the laws of no man. They had cars, somehow, and drugs, somehow, and most of all they had a pervasive sense of entitled freedom. They could come and go as they pleased. They didn't belong to Oberlin. They belonged to the world. Well, not the world exactly, but Providence, Hartford, Meadowlands, Red Rocks, Irvine, Berkeley.

They were also enormously, famously stupid.

One of them, a frizzy-haired brunette, asked me as we brushed our teeth in the dorm's communal women's bathroom, "So, you live with Fred?"

"And how!" I replied, because I loved my roommate.

"Wait, you have two roommates?"

To be honest, it all looked sort of enviable to me: the annual escape, the happiness, the tie-dye so pervasive and rainbowlike that it ceased being color altogether and became an especially jolly kind of brown. Even the stupidity. When the Deadheads came back from Tour, flaunting stories of their exploits as they wolfed tempeh scramble, I eyed them with a kind of grudging admiration. Nobody was that simple. They had to be faking it.

U Is for the Unknown

I did not want to go on tour, but I did want to hit the road. I had a growing apprehension that all this was not for me. In the end, I dropped out. In fact, I dropped out of Oberlin not once but twice. I wearied of it all and quit and then like a moron went back a year later to make sure it still wearied me and it did. I couldn't be in that cornfield terrarium without hating myself and everyone else. So I left, to do I knew not what. But I turned my back on my middle-class birthright of ease and premade decisions. I don't say this with pride or with any sense of sneering superiority over those who stuck it out. I wish I'd had their ability to understand the structure of what was occurring: We were in an idyll. We were pulling ourselves together before we went out in the world.

But I couldn't see that, or didn't feel I deserved it. I was impelled from Oberlin. I simply couldn't understand how everyone could stay put here, in their carrels and at their parties and in their shabby off-campus houses where they scrupulously took turns doing dishes.

V Is for Vintage Contemporaries

Okay, so I wanted to be a writer. I had no idea how to go about it. In March I applied to the Oberlin creative writing program but was denied entry because the director didn't like my attitude. He said I was too critical. Well, there wasn't anything I could do about *that*. If I was blackballed from the creative writing program, how the fuck was I going to become a writer? I was going to have to rely on books, I guessed, like I always had. On my windowsill they were lined up: the books for my classes at school, and alongside them the beloved books I'd brought from home. There was my copy of *Fin-de-siècle Vienna* by Carl Schorske, given to me by my high-school history teacher. Well, lent to me by my high-school history teacher, but it was so pretty with its gold cover that I simply kept it. I told myself that owning the Schorske meant I was interested in European history, but really I just liked to get myself worked up looking at the surprisingly dirty Klimt reproductions. There was my row of Penguins; the necessary (to me) frivolities of Mitford and Waugh and Wodehouse. And there were my Vintage Contemporaries: Raymond Carver, Joy Williams, Frederick Exley, Jay McInerney, Richard

Ford. I would buy and read anything with that echt-'80s design on the cover. It was the word "contemporary," I think, that was really important to me. These people were writing now.

At my high school and all through my first year of Oberlin, I'd been taught to read for meaning and subtext and symbol. I was good at it. I read with a facile "I solved it!" seriousness. I didn't know it but I was a product of the New School criticism that still ruled English departments at that time. Somehow along the way, I'd forgotten how to read properly, the way I'd read as a kid. If I'd been reading with real, heartfelt, childish seriousness, I could've learned all about being a writer right there in my cozy room with Fred. I could've learned from the books on my shelf. It was, after all, right there on page 37 of *A Fan's Notes:* "literature is born out of the very longing I was so seeking to repress."

W Is for Weird

Everyone at Oberlin was the weirdest person from his or her senior class in high school. Now picture all these weirdos in a cornfield, with no diversions except our own weirdness and our sordid knowledge we hadn't gotten into Brown. There was the boy who collected his nail clippings in a pickle jar. There was the girl who'd famously tasted all her bodily secretions. Only at Oberlin would that be a cause for fame. These weirdos were united by their shared and overwhelming desire to become modern dancers. The backup plan? A sensible career in anthropology. I myself was the second-weirdest kid from my high-school senior class (the weirdest was Vanessa, now at Bennington), and while I had no interest in modern dance, I had written more than my fair share of poetry, which is like modern dance for uncoordinated people.

A Is for Acid: An Oberlin Abecedarium

X Is for XX Chromosomes

My friend Elizabeth kissed me in the bathroom at a party. She was getting ready to become a lesbian and was tired of waiting around. "Let's get it over with!" she exclaimed under the buzzing fluorescent bathroom light, and smooched me. What I remember is how tiny her mouth was. Her lips were somehow more *precise* than a boy's. So that happened. A few weeks later one of the famous lesbians ran her hand down my neck at the disco.

Cassie, she of the cool affect and the staring nipples, struck up a conversation with me after a Fred Astaire movie, and we became acquaintances. She was a glamorous acquaintance to have, and I was perfectly content with things as they stood. Then her notes started appearing in my campus mailbox. These notes were written in an angular, slanting, black-inked script and asked me to do things, like take a walk or go out for a milk shake or whatever. But the notes were really asking me, in a vintage, black-and-white, restrained way, to have sex. I could tell.

We began to see each other every day. She told me stories of what she'd been up to in San Francisco, stories that reminded me of the life I'd left behind in Seattle, the urban life I missed so much. She was a selfish romantic like me. One night we walked across campus, breaking off dogwood boughs and piling them in our arms. "Let's put them in my room," she said. We went to her room, which was entirely devoid of decoration in a way that all but announced "What a dump!" She'd had the good taste not to attempt to mitigate the cinder-block shittiness of dorm life. We piled the flowers on the desk and she turned and kissed me on the mouth. Some little motor seemed to start in her then, and she all but pushed me down on the bed. In bed, her waifishness fell entirely away and she had me out of my pants in about ten seconds, and had her head between my legs almost as quickly.

We had a lot of sex that spring, though I was still nominally dating Matthew, whatever *that* meant. He had always been withholding, so there wasn't a big change when I began to spend all my time with Cassie, learning what it's really like Down There. I liked the badness of it, but felt a curious sense of detachment from the sex act itself. What I really wanted to learn was her coolness, her remove, her ability to seem as if she didn't care. She would fling herself at me, practically tear my clothes off, send me out of my head with her little fingers, and then roll over afterward and look at me with cool Antonioni eyes, like, *Who are you again?*

The spring grew hotter and more fecund-smelling. We lay in bed one night in late May, saying goodbye. She was getting ready to go back to San Francisco, to spend the summer with a despised stepmother, the latest in a string.

"Are you going to see Matthew this summer?" she asked.

"Probably," I said. "I hope."

And she started to cry, and I was so surprised.

Y Is for "You Spin Me Round (Like a Record)"

Matthew liked to put on eye makeup and go dancing. See, that was the thing about Matthew, you just never knew. You'd think he was all violin-practicing sobriety and then he'd bust out the hair spray. Fred and I had a disco night we deejayed. We called our disco night "How Do You Solve a Problem Like Maria?" and Matthew came and danced, his hair moussed ridiculously. His dancing was a kind of tribute. No matter what I put on, he danced, harder and harder—"Strawberry Letter 23," "Takin' Care of Business," "How Soon Is Now?"—until finally at the end of the night I put on "You Spin Me Round" and joined him on the floor, where he was sweaty and deeply uncool. I really loved him. I know that now, thirty years later. That's a nice thing about being middle-aged—it's very obvious whom you really did love, and who was merely a giant distraction or an elaborate form of self-abuse. I really loved Matthew, and sometimes I think that's the only good thing I got out of Oberlin, and sometimes I think that's enough. It turns out you just don't get to love that many people in that tidal, self-obliterating kind of way. I think maybe I was lucky to go to Oberlin, to find someone to love for a little while.

But, honestly, it was time to leave. You can't pay that kind of tuition just to love someone.

Z Is for Zinn

We have come to the end, and my studies have made the briefest appearance. Let us turn to them now, determinedly. The class that really mattered to me was Popular Piety, taught by a professor named Grover Zinn, who had a cube-shaped head and a rhetorical style generously described as linear. Zinn lectured us about the lives of the saints. The saints were characters with stories. I found these stories more literary and more immediately relevant to my panicked life than the poems of Williams and Stevens and Jeffers that we were reading in Modern American Poetry. Poems I could explain—I could and did halt the entire class's discussion of "Thirteen Ways of Looking at a Blackbird" with a swift, contemptuous exegesis. But the saints baffled and moved me. They resisted explanation; they were pure feeling, pure tragedy. They were like superheroes: Saint Catherine hoist on the spiked wheel; Hildegard of Bingen with her visions that terrified her; Saint Clare, protégée of Saint Francis, who practiced extreme poverty and inspired a group of acolytes called Poor Clares. My people!

Popular Piety met in Peters Hall, the insistently vertical Gothic pile on the edge of the busy, social quad. But our classroom faced away from the quad and its hive, overlooking instead the verdancy of Tappan Square, where treetops obscured the grass below. I found the whole scene intensely consoling: the methodical nature of Zinn's speech; the view of the waving, hushing elm-tops; and most of all the saints, who made suffering into a form of devotion.

October 1988, age twenty-one

I'm not in school and I can't work there and I don't know what's to become of me. I can always write I guess. It's useless to pretend that I'm not going there almost solely to see R (and it's an "adventure") and I have a hard time putting that much importance on it. On what? On love I guess. Scary.

14.

Repulsion!

In December 1988 I found myself the resident of the second-most-dangerous street in Australia. Or so I was told by the girl serving coffee at Badde Manors, a café on a prominent corner of Sydney's Glebe Point Road. I was twenty-one years old, unemployed, and not even really sure where I was exactly. But I knew how to drink coffee. Or maybe not, as I discovered when I ordered a latte in my American accent.

"What's a latte?" asked the coffee girl.

"It's espresso and steamed milk. Is that not what it's called here?"

"I think what you want is a flat white. Are you backpacking?"

"No, I'm living in Sydney for a bit."

"Really. Where you staying?"

"Redfern."

"What!?" But she said it "Wha" or, really, "Whaaauuuh?" She gaped at me. "Redfern? What street?"

"George Street."

"That's the worst street in Sydney. Well, probably Redfern Street is the worst street in Sydney. But George has got to be the second-worst street."

She steamed milk, looked thoughtful, and then yelled over the animal roar of the espresso machine, "And if it's the second-worst street in Sydney, it's the second-worst street in Australia. What are you doing there?"

"My boyfriend is a professor at Sydney Uni. He says it's affordable."

"Oh, I'll wager it's affordable, all right. You should move. He can stay, but you need to get out of there."

I took my coffee to a table and got out my book: *The Fatal Shore,* by Robert Hughes, a history of Australia whose title I varied in my mind to *The Largest Bore, the Hardest Snore.* I found it hard to concentrate. The second-worst street in Australia. It had a disturbingly specific sound to it.

How had I come to find myself in this situation? After I dropped out of Oberlin, not once but twice, I had moved home to Seattle and fallen in love with a physics professor from New Zealand who was about fifteen years older than me. He was teaching at the University of Washington; I found him in a café and then a bar and he had red hair and a strong nose and tendony forearms and was so, so handsome. He pressed his number on me in a stern way, as if forbidding me ever to use it. If Schlegelian irony is something that's given and taken back at the same time, well, that's exactly how the physicist gave me his phone number. He walked up to me at the Comet Tavern, told me I was beautiful, handed me his phone number, and all the while made me feel I had done something wrong. His approach was perfectly judged.

He had studied collider physics and had jockeyed (not his verb) the particle accelerator at Fermilab, the big, famous laboratory near Chicago, and so my friends (home from college for the summer, not dropouts like me) named him the Quark Basher. They looked on, I imagine, in horror as I determinedly fell in love. Why the Quark Basher? Who knows? I didn't even

like him. He was censorious and moralistic. Not in an interesting way but in that boring way that hates Americans. "You eat
in cars! That's uncivilized." Like Josephine, I suppose I wanted
to test myself and he presented a challenge.

The Quark Basher was getting ready to move to Australia—he
had taken a job at Sydney University. I felt pulled to go with.
Maybe I just liked him because he was a geographic catapult,
flinging me from one continent to another.

In September, he went ahead, to work in a lab in the out-
back (bashing required a lot of space) and to find us a place to
live in Sydney. I stayed behind, took some classes at the University of Washington, and worked a lot of hours at a coffeehouse
to make some money. I found myself very interested in my writing class. This was something I could do, wanted to do, in fact
was obsessed with doing. And so I left it and fled for the other
side of the world.

My mom thought it was funny that I took a train to Australia. She made lots of jokes about the geographical ineptitude of
the gesture. I took the train to San Francisco (the plane ticket
to Sydney from there was notably cheaper than the ticket from
Seattle). When I got there, I stayed for a week, over the course
of which I made out with not one but two ex-boyfriends (not at
the same time) on the sidewalks of the Mission District, which
probably should have forewarned me about the longevity of my
relationship with the Quark Basher.

Nonetheless, full of drinks and kisses and doubts, I made
my flight and fourteen hours later landed in Sydney. Usually I
was thoughtless and easygoing when I traveled, but this time I
had the mother of all stomachaches. I think now of John Cheever's line from "The Jewels of the Cabots": "The sense that what
we part from forcibly and with deep regret is what we love and
know best and our departure is impetuous, visionary, and dangerous." My departure for college hadn't had this sense of dan-

ger, this quality of schism. College was such the accepted thing to do that I might as well have had my mother pack me a lunch and lay out my Garanimals for me. This was the real deal. The austral. Clearly I wanted to get away from something, and in retrospect it's obvious it was myself.

I arrived at Sydney International early in the morning, with my big duffel bag full of books and holey T-shirts and my diaphragm in its plastic case. Even inside the terminal, even at the start of the day, the light was white and blinding and clean-seeming. He was waiting for me on the other side of customs. He wore a perfect plain white poplin shirt and black Carhartts. Everything about him was plain, stripped-down. He kissed me with his gorgeous lips, the hooked lips of a salmon, and threw my bag in the back of his truck, which he called his "ute." It belonged to the university, which he called the "uni," and he had borrowed it for the day.

The Basher was in his mid-thirties. Being with an older man made me feel my youth—which, let's face it, was so often a burden—as a kind of material good. When I was with other people my own age, my youth was invisible. We were all the same; youth is a relative notion. But set against his oldness, my youth itself became a fetish or a beauty mark. An older man was authoritative, and that was what I secretly wanted, someone to tell me what to do—the way the short-story writer would make me his passenger all those long years later.

"On the way home," he said, "I want to take you out to the bush. I want you to see it." He persisted in a belief that I was a nature girl because I rode a bicycle and liked above all things to swim in open bodies of water. He put the car into gear and pulled out of the parking lot, onto the blazing straight black asphalt highway. He didn't ask what I wanted to do, which was brush my teeth. We drove to a park with some eucalyptus trees and some reddish dirt and a lot of low bushes. There was no grass, just an open field that contained these things: the trees, the dirt, the bushes. Sky. I was blurred with plane fatigue. There was a soft, furry, overripe taste in my mouth. He opened the back of the ute and drew out a canvas bag. We sat at a picnic table and he produced from the bag two baguette sandwiches, some fruit, some wine, and a corkscrew.

He told me about his lab, didn't ask about my writing class. "So," he said, after a while, "I'm going to head home to New Zealand for Christmas. To see my parents."

Christmas was just a couple of weeks away. I noted the use of first-person singular. "You are?" I asked. "Like, just you?"

"They'd be shocked," he said. "You're so young. It wouldn't be right for them to meet you." He was simply thinking of their well-being. "It would be awkward," he said. I looked at him in disbelief. I had flown out here, on the strength of what exactly? His beautiful face? The way he smelled like an apricot? His impeccable musical taste? His large penis? My idiocy was suddenly clear to me.

"I really, really need to brush my teeth," I said. "Could you please take me to the house?" I couldn't bring myself to call it home.

"Of course," he said. "We need to get you settled and comfortable and happy." He said it as though this was obvious, as though I were the one who had insisted on this picnic among the unpicturesque shrubberies.

We folded up the waxed paper from our sandwiches and put it in the canvas bag for a further use. He did not like waste. Then we climbed in the ute and headed into Sydney.

In the city, away from the oppressive, beautiful sky, I began to feel better. We approached from the south, the ugliest approach to Sydney. But the low rows of businesses and semidetached houses with their red roofs seemed friendly to me. A vacuum-repair shop, something called a milk bar, a check-cashing place. The nimble little white ute sped along the road, stripped-down and sensible.

"Are you okay?" he asked. We had that kind of talk, the kind so filled with silence that one person had occasionally to lob a volley to the other, just to check on them.

"Tired," I said, from the wrong side of the car on the wrong side of the road, and looked out the wrong window. We drove through a vibrant, bohemian-seeming neighborhood called Newtown, and then through another, still more quaint, called Glebe, and I began to cheer up. I understood these landscapes. Bookshops and pubs and Italian restaurants. We kept driving, though, into a series of tough gray concrete lanes, devoid of charm or even, it seemed, of businesses.

He pulled up in front of a terrace house. These houses were all linked together, cheek by jowl, like town houses. They had flat façades to the street on the bottom floor and iron grillwork on the top floor. They were pretty and unusual and obviously vernacular. (I had learned this word in an architectural history class at Oberlin.) But the street was dirty, strewn with garbage, and eerily empty. There was no street life, no corner store.

He swung the door open and I stepped inside an entirely empty room. We passed through its bareness into another room, this with a long table and two folding chairs. A copy of Antonio Gramsci's *Prison Notebooks* (I'm not kidding) sat on the table, along with that day's newspaper and some physics journals.

The kitchen was empty of any convenience, including a refrigerator. There was a stove top and a sink and a window, and aside from that a linoleum emptiness. It was revealed that the Quark Basher kept all food, including dairy products, in a wooden cabinet. This at the beginning of Sydney's hot summer. Well, what did I know? Refrigeration was probably one of those conveniences that crass Americans were overreliant upon.

Upstairs were two rooms, one that overlooked the street and

featured a bed hung all around with mosquito netting, which fit pleasantly with my idea of what I was here for. Or maybe gave me an idea. We had sex. We did it on his bed; we never had sex anywhere other than his bed. Ever. He was like one of those people who can take a dump only at their own house, except with sex. It was nice enough, though the light was sad in that small, brick-walled upstairs room in the middle of that big, strange city.

Then I lay there idly while he went down to the kitchen. Someone in a house nearby was playing the violin. It was December, and hot. The Quark Basher had no fan. A fan would've been excessive. This, after all, was a man who prided himself on being able to keep a clean house with only a bucket and a brush. Or something. I wouldn't know, I never cleaned his house. It would never have occurred to me to intrude on his systems thusly. Back in Seattle, I had once washed the dishes and he immediately rewashed them.

He came upstairs with a little cup of dark, grainy espresso that he had made in his octagonal stove-top pot. I had gotten to know this device in his Seattle apartment and had an appropriate terror of it. An espresso pot like that meant something in those days: that you were a serious person.

He handed the cup to me. "Shall we walk over to Sydney Uni?" he said. "It's very close by. That's why this place is such a find. People say this neighborhood is rough, but that's just because Australians are so backward that they're afraid of the Aborigines." A classic one-way rivalry: Kiwis hated Aussies; Aussies, I would find out later, rarely could be bothered to think about Kiwis.

We walked to Sydney Uni along gray streets, arriving suddenly at its green swards and red bricks. Young people, people my age, were everywhere, with their beautiful skin and funny outfits. Sydney Uni was the best university in Australia; these were my people. Well raised, beloved, stuffed with education.

Repulsion!

How come I now found myself in extremis, a kind of liminal figure, a mistress, a fetish, something disposable and embarrassing? I had a funny feeling I'd done this to myself, but wasn't sure exactly how.

The next couple of weeks passed pleasantly enough. We explored the city by foot. Sometimes the Basher would laugh at the way I walked: tilted forward into my stride, always leading with my chin. "You're so *determined*," he said.

He was right, I *was* determined, but to do what I had no idea. I'd reached some kind of nadir. No prospects of college. No job, and getting low on dough. A hankering to write that made me feel afraid and embarrassed. And this stupid boyfriend who was handsome and brilliant and who clearly lusted for me but who, I feared, really did not like me very much.

We walked forth every day into the full sunshiny glory of Sydney, making our way eastward until we came, by foot and bus (but why couldn't we just borrow the ute from the uni?) to Tamarama, Bondi's more esoteric sister beach, where we swam and swam until I was crunchy with salt and brown from the sun.

Tamarama was like the setting for some Forsterian crisis of the self. The beach made a little half circle, pushing up against the massive, looming rocks. The place had a South Seas brutalism that was a shock to encounter right in the middle of this cosmopolitan belle of a city. It was hard, in teeming Sydney, to remember that you were on the edge of a vast and mostly unpopulated continent. Tamarama was more like the rest of Australia, with intimations of infinitude from which the mind recoiled a bit. The waves rolled steeply into the beach.

In the temperate water I didn't quite think anymore but lost myself, drifted out toward larger currents, grew stronger and stronger and dumber and dumber.

At night we went out to hear bands and drink beers—the

only things we had in common were punk rock and swimming in the ocean. Both activities that didn't involve talking, you might note.

In between bands, we'd argue. The Basher's main theme was making sure that I understood that everyone hated Americans. (And of course I must never say "America." Only "the U.S."—or, better still, "the States"—would do.)

When I asked for ketchup with my fish-and-chips, he would elbow me: "Tomato sauce," he'd hiss, on guard against my nascent cultural imperialism.

Eventually we had to make our way back to Redfern. We walked through its dark streets briskly; while the Basher maintained a show-offy insouciance about Redfern and its dangers, I noticed his pace quickened on those late-night strolls back to our terrace house. Once home we would have sex and lie inside our netting listening to mosquitoes buzzing around the room. As the night wore on, we heard other sounds too. Crashing glass, yelling, what sounded like garbage cans being tipped over. And sounds came closer; banging on our windows and door, hysterical laughter on our doorstep. The seventh night I was there, I left my bag downstairs. In the morning it and my passport were gone. I spent three days at the consulate replacing it. In my new passport photo I looked sullen and very, very tan.

I met a couple of his friends from Sydney Uni—a physicist, Wilfred, and his (age-appropriate) girlfriend, Jill, who lived in a more comprehensible way over in Newtown, in familiar-feeling group-house squalor. They had us over for dinner. I felt happy there as we batted a cricket ball in the back garden. The garden was narrow and hemmed in by other houses, and the sun slanted across just one corner.

Wilfred tossed the ball gently to me, and I experimentally batted away at it. As he pitched, he asked, "Will you be studying while you're here?"

I colored. "I don't have a student visa."

Pretty, petite, age-appropriate Jill asked, "Will you be working, then?" She seemed to be keeping a close eye on Wilfred.

I'd been saving money for months to come here because I knew I couldn't work, at least over the table, in Australia. "Actually I don't have a working visa either. I want to travel." That sounded good. "But I'm going to need to work, somehow or another, so if you hear of anything . . ." They assured me they'd let me know.

The Basher said, pointedly, "To get a work visa in Oz, you need to have some kind of skill."

We didn't invite Wilfred and Jill to our place.

And then it was the week before Christmas, and he was gone. I walked the streets, just as the Basher and I had done, but now it was different. I had liked following him all around town, subsuming my own desires like crazy. I was heliotropic in the extreme. Now I just wandered.

Out and about I tried not to look at or speak to anyone. I wasn't nervous about them hurting me, I was nervous about me hurting them—with my horrible American-ness. The QB had so terrified me about this that I barely ever spoke above a whisper and tried not to set my hegemonic, overly frank Yankee gaze directly at any Aussie. They didn't strike me as exactly shrinking violets. Things they seemed to like: the Ramones, short shorts for men, chocolate milk. These proclivities didn't bespeak a refinement that would be troubled by a little thing like an American accent, but even so I whispered my way around town.

When I needed to rest, I made my way not home but to the grand State Library of New South Wales, an imposing cream-colored pile on Macquarie Street. There were books, and a spare, elegant café, and other readers. I began to make my way through Tolstoy; I found his multitudinousness a good antidote to the emptiness of my new life. There was a sweetness and a purpose to my solitude in the library. Late in the afternoon I had to exit the cool gray dim into the hot afternoon and make my way back to Redfern. If I didn't get home before six o'clock or so, I would have to take a cab that I could ill afford—I couldn't walk around my neighborhood after dark.

A couple of days before Christmas, I walked across the city to the tony, boho neighborhood of Paddington. The art-house cinema there was showing *Repulsion.*

It wasn't a long walk to Paddington, though it might have been light-years away in terms of how much the cityscape changed. I started out my journey amid the barebones amenities of my own neighborhood and an hour later found myself in Paddo: folk-music shops, pubs with gourmet food, fish-and-chips places immaculately tiled and recalling Brighton in their Englishness, hat stores quaintly calling themselves "milliners" (there was a trend that year for broad-brimmed straw hats with crowns banded by grosgrain, rather Lucy Honeychurch-ish, actually; I coveted one).

I made my way up the street; I was starting to get hungry and headed for the fish-and-chips place at the far end of the road. In my mind I rehearsed saying "tomato sauce" instead of "ketchup." As I made my determined way up the street, a group of men spilled noisily out of a pub just ahead.

My first impression was that they were all young and handsome and blond and somehow entitled-looking. This made them scarier—it also seemed very cinematic. They were gorgeous thugs, as if *A Clockwork Orange* had been recast with Ralph Lauren models. Before I knew what was happening, they were around me and hands were everywhere. Up my dress, on my legs, in my hair, in my bag, on my cheek, grabbing, finding holds

and crevices and grabbing. All I could think was that I didn't
want them to know I was American. I knew that if they knew
I was American, it would turn to full-on rape. I thought, This is
crazy. It's sunshiny. It's the middle of a Sunday afternoon. No
one is stopping. I mustered my best Aussie rip-off voice and
said over and over "Fuck right off!" I got my elbows and knees
going, and started pushing. They pushed back, harder. How
many were there? Memory has the count at, like, eight, but it
could've been three or twelve. More than two. More than two is
a mob, in that particular situation, a thing I now knew.

I thought, If I can just get my momentum going again, I'll
be up the street, it'll all be over, and I'll be gone again. In flight.
And that's just what happened—I was expelled, I expelled
myself from the group and I was halfway up the block, feeling
bruises rise on my thighs and my neck. I know bruises don't
really come that fast, but I felt purple. I kept walking. I didn't
know where to go, or what to do.

Catherine Deneuve walks alone through the city. Every eye
seems to be on her, but she's terrified. Every man is, to her, a
potential assault. She is walking toward an empty apartment in
a strange city. Deneuve's character, Carol, is a French girl living
in London with her sister and working, quite indifferently, as a
beautician, though every touch of the flesh is a mortification to
her. She's as perfect and pale and cool as a vanilla milk shake,
but any whiff of sex makes her cringe with anxiety. When her
sister goes away with a married lover on vacation, Carol is left
alone.

Isolated by her living situation, her language, even by her
very beauty, Carol tries at first to go to work and to navigate
around the city like a normal person. But soon she barricades
herself in her flat, where she battles an imaginary intruder,

watches a skinned rabbit rot (probably how most British people of the era imagined French people spending their spare hours anyway), stares dully into space, crawls around naked, and eventually ends up killing two men.

I sat there in Paddo, shaking. The movie unspooled scene after scene of unnerving violence, but the scariest parts, for me, were the images not of the killings but of Carol's aloneness, her wanderings of the streets and then her prowlings of her apartment, unsure of where to go or what to do, unsure of where she might belong. Fucking Polanski, looking at her, lingering on her discomfort. And yet he didn't just make her a victim. He turned her into a monster too.

Alone in my house, all too aware I was reenacting the solitude of that other C.D., I heard the violin playing again. Also: clanging metal and loud voices. Years later, this street would be the scene of the worst race riots in Australian history. I lay in bed, trying to read inside my white mosquito net, a girl in a cloud. The sounds seemed so nearby, as though the house itself were made from net. I needed to get drunk, but there was no alcohol in the house except a bit of wine. And I couldn't go out. There was no phone, so I couldn't have called a cab even if I had wanted to. I lay like that, in my whitish shroud, thinking about skinned rabbits and also wishing my hair would lie flat like Catherine Deneuve's until finally it was morning and time to boil coffee in the terrifying little pot.

I opened the kitchen door to the tiny little patch of concrete that made the back garden, and sat on the ground, and administered myself a dose of yesterday's newspaper.

I read every word of the previous day's news and then made my way to the cupboard, where I got out the unrefrigerated eggs. I whisked two with a little water and sautéed them on the hot plate with a soft, maybe rancid, lump of butter and a few chopped scallions.

I walked up to the main road and caught the bus to Bondi Junction, and from there to Bondi Beach. I walked the cliffside trail to Tamarama. I watched the couples kissing. I bodysurfed alone, surely one of the stupidest things a human can do. I walked up to the shop and bought some candy and a Victoria Bitter and took it all back to the beach and drank the beer. I hadn't eaten since the eggs, and I gnawed on some chocolate. I ran a comb through my hair. I felt the tops of my cheekbones turning red. I didn't want to go back to the house. I was afraid of what I would find there, afraid I wouldn't have enough books or beers to get through the night.

On Christmas Day I walked to the botanical gardens. Flying foxes, which looked as though they should not be airborne or perhaps shouldn't even exist, swooped overhead, among what I supposed might be gum trees. I went home that night and cut out Christmasy shapes—trees, bells, even an attempt at an angel or two—from the newspaper and glued them with spermicidal jelly to the brick wall of the dining room. I stopped and considered my work, then added some flying foxes. I dreamed of disappearing and leaving the glued-up shapes as an obscure message for the Basher.

A couple of days later—weary of swimming and of eggs and even of Natasha Rostova—in a fit of self-preservation I went to a record store and determinedly chatted up the owner, who was a fan of all things Seattle, this before everyone, or even anyone, was a fan of all things Seattle. He put me on the list for a New Year's Eve show at the Lansdowne Hotel. The headliner was a band called the Hard-Ons. "Motorhead meets the Beach Boys," promised the record-store guy. It was good to be on a list.

On New Year's Eve, I dressed carefully in cutoff Levi's shorts, Docs, a sleeveless lace blouse that had belonged to my granny in the 1960s, a plaid flannel shirt, stacks of leather cat collars on my arms. I looked, in my own estimation, very cute. If there was one thing I knew (and it's possible there was in fact only one thing), it was how to get dressed for a rock show.

I left my house at about five o'clock. As always, there didn't seem to be anyone on the street—it was like a fucking Chirico painting. Long afternoon shadows fell against cement street and brick walls. I had to get out, into a better neighborhood, before dark. I set aside some taxi fare for the trip home, a little investment in my future. I would try not to drink too much.

I made my way toward the address the record-store guy had given me. I was very early, and if I arrived now I would just embarrass myself and everyone else. I knew of a nearby book-shop and went there and sat on one of those round squat rolling stools and tried to read Patrick White. It seemed like the right thing to do, reading an important Australian writer, but it was very dull. After an hour or two, I walked toward the pub, hoping that the streets wouldn't be filled with rapist Aryan thugs. As I nervously toed my way along I saw a figure up ahead: long hair, leather jacket, cutoff jeans like mine, Chucks. A boy. I'd been stuck with this mean old man, and then alone in my house, and here was a boy, the very thing I required.

I—softly, politely—asked where the Lansdowne might be. I couldn't think of a way to disguise my American-ness.

"You're a Yank!" he said with delight.

"I am."

"Excellent. Let me walk you to the pub." Someone liked me, or at least liked my nationality! Up close I saw that he wore a Flamin' Groovies T-shirt and he was bow-lipped, big-eyed: really beautiful.

Sydney at this time was host to a muscular, heroin-fueled

rock scene that specialized in a combination of heaviness and silliness—the Hard-Ons were in some ways the perfect Sydney band: scary and funny. I didn't know any of that when I walked into the Lansdowne, of course. I just knew that the place was packed with leather-jacketed guys who looked like they were trying out for a spot in the Stooges circa 1970. Not a few had that distinctive dope pallor that is impossible to (a) cover up or (b) fake. There were scarcely any women or girls, and among the ones I saw, a tarted-up aesthetic seemed to apply: lots of tight black velvet, patterned stockings, etc.; rock chick as hooker. There was, I thought, a smell of vomit.

My sweet, cute escort was named Dave and was in a band and of course knew Chris Dunn, the record-store guy.

"Dunny," called Dave, pushing dark curls out of his face.

"Drinks!" said Chris. "My shout."

Dave and I chatted—about our moms, of all things, though his was a mum—while Chris got our bevvies. I had asked for a vodka cranberry, and he handed me two. "That way we don't have to fight our way to the bar when it's time for another." Ah, the real Oz at last.

I mentioned the vomit smell.

"Oh yeah," said Chris. "That's cause this pub has been redone, carpeted and that. Harder to get the smell out." The old pubs were all tiled, all over the floor, up the sides of the bar itself, up the walls, so they could just hose the place down at the end of the night. "A good system, wasn't it?"

The rest of the night was pretty pro forma. Dave stayed by my side, chatting easily and offering to drive me home—he had a car. Yes! I could drink my taxi fare! We got back to my place and I didn't ask him in. Which meant I liked him, and he knew it. His own band—he was the singer—was playing an afternoon show the next day in a pub on the north end of town. I could take the train there. As it happened, it was one of the old-fashioned pubs that was still tiled all over. "So you can vomit as much as you like!"

We embraced and kissed, a promise.

I went into the house and could feel something was wrong. There was a draft coming from the kitchen, but I knew the window there was painted shut, and also had bars over it. I walked slowly in. I was back in *Repulsion,* had passed from the world into my isolation as quickly as I had walked from Dave's Holden station wagon to my front door.

The kitchen window had been broken. Shards of glass and syringes lay scattered across the floor. Lots of syringes, spilling blood onto my kitchen floor. I made myself look at the scene. I pieced together what had probably happened: Someone or more likely several someones had climbed over the wall into our tiny back garden/prison yard, spent some blissful minutes or hours booting dope (New Year's Eve!), and then broken the pane, hoping they could reach from the window to the latch on the back door. Failing that objective, they'd chucked their works into my (really the Quark Basher's) kitchen—perhaps in a gesture of hostility at our whiteness, our non-belonging—and made off into the night.

I couldn't go outside. I couldn't call a cab—no phone. I leaned into the kitchen and pulled two warm cans of Victoria Bitter from the cupboard, along with a flaccid chocolate bar. I climbed the stairs wearily and got inside my white shroud. I opened *War and Peace* and began to read.

October 4, 1989, age twenty-two

Last night I dreamt I was late for school—and how!

15

Syllabus

I had been planless for so long. I had become one of those girls my dad so annoyingly called "lost souls." Why were boys never lost souls, only girls? Though my dad used the term metaphorically, I was literally lost, traveling from one end of the earth to another, ending up, finally, in a little beachfront house at the foot of the Illawarra escarpment. I'd never even heard of Illawarra or an escarpment before, and now here I was, living in the shadow of the Illawarra escarpment. It hovered dramatically over me, making me feel like it, the Illawarra escarpment, meant something, or maybe like my life meant something. But none of it meant anything at all. I was just experiencing an exciting geographic proximity.

It was a sweet existence in many ways. I had my loving and beautiful boyfriend Dave, who was sort of a rock star and also the nicest boyfriend I'd ever had. I had work—nude modeling and shifting boxes in a warehouse, not at the same time. There were shows and beaches and long days filled with nothing but reading. When I got restless or Dave was on tour, I hopped trains up and down the coast with a couple of daredevil pals I'd made. But I knew I was supposed to be a student. I wrote in my diary:

"Last night I dreamt I was late for school—and how!" Which was funny, but I didn't feel funny. I felt like I was twenty-two and a college dropout twice over and getting older every day in the wrong hemisphere. I truly believed I would live outside bourgeois society for the rest of my days, nude modeling and warehouse laboring. Maybe I would get promoted to forklift driver. There was nothing in me that believed that the normal things that happened to normal people were things that were going to happen to me. I looked like a free girl—after all, I stuck my thumb out and hitchhiked all the way to Queensland—but at this point I believed I was worthless, pretty much, except maybe my looks, and I don't think a worthless-feeling person is a free person. I read exhaustively. From Tolstoy I'd moved on to Virginia Woolf and James Joyce and Thomas Mann and, of all people, Doris Lessing, who made me think in uncomfortably explicit ways about girls and freedom, and the difficulty of the novels was the only thing keeping me from falling into total despair. My brain was a little hammer, looking for somewhere to fall.

Finally the decision was made for me: Australia kicked me out. My tourist visa, re-upped again and again, was denied, and I was summarily sent back to the States. I made a months-long pit stop in San Francisco. I loved the Mission District, where I lived in a spacious sunny old apartment. I worked at the magnificent vegetarian restaurant Greens, strode around the city in my big boots, went to the Japanese bathhouse, acquired a girlfriend, and generally enjoyed what would turn out to be the last flowering of SF's affordable bohemia. But ultimately I was no more Californian than I was Ohioan or Australian, and I went home to Seattle. And there at last, I got down to business. I found a dumb job at a gift shop and a little basement apartment a few miles from where I'd grown up. And I enrolled in UW.

I was twenty-three and perceived myself as quite ancient, a battered artifact of another era. I was starting school in winter quarter. The day before classes began, I rode my bike over to campus just to have a look around. It was cold and drizzly. My leather book bag swung heavily around to the front of my torso as I hunched over my handlebars. A Dinosaur Jr. cassette played on my Walkman and I rode in loose circles across campus, checking out all the buildings that housed all the departments: forestry, physics, engineering. I would never take a class in any of these buildings, but there they were. There was a golden, infinite feeling I had never felt at Oberlin. Of course it had nothing to do with UW and everything to do with me and my readiness to begin to learn. I had traveled the wide world and found that that was its own finitude.

I chose a major called, really, comparative history of ideas. We read Edward Said and Thomas Kuhn, and we did our best with Hegel and Schopenhauer and Kierkegaard and all the way back to Plato. I had no real talent for this kind of thinking—it wasn't like English class, where I could say a few words about Ezra Pound and shut everyone the fuck up. In my CHID classes, I rarely spoke up, and when I did, the kinder students and professors moved the conversation along quickly because what I'd said was generally so rudimentary as to be an embarrassment to all. I liked that. I liked the heights. It was snowy and alpine up there, and even if my comprehension wasn't perfect, my head felt *clear,* possibly for the first time since I was a little kid. I grew more and more silent in the seminar rooms; my professors regarded my term papers with something like amazement; I had been thinking all along? I'd given no sign of it.

My apartment was silent too. I was a little lonely. When spring came, I grew cosmos in my window box. I did a lot of elaborate, buttery baking. Butter, in fact, was my main food. I made polenta every night, dropping huge knobs of butter and cheese into the bubbling gold, and I wondered why I was getting SO FAT. I was finally gaining the freshman fifteen, five years too late. Butter was my best companion.

Syllabus

A high-school friend, living alone in Paris, wrote that she too was lonely. She told me she hung a sewing needle tied to a thread from the center of the ceiling of her single room. The needle dangled there, just below eye level. She said it helped her concentrate her thoughts and gave her a feeling of companionship, something to navigate around. I tried it too, and left the needle there for a few weeks, where it reminded me of this comrade in loneliness, far away in France.

Sometimes I went out with old friends from high school to the loudest rock shows we could find—very loud indeed in Seattle in 1990—and drank myself into oblivion. I learned a new kind of drinking, assertive and with the goal of blacking out. Occasionally, out on the town, I accidentally fucked someone or other—whoops! More than occasionally, truth be told. In fact, I developed a knack for full-on true-blue for-realz one-night stands, the kind where there was no promise of further connection. In fact, I fought further connection. If, like Josephine, my goal previously had been world domination one man at a time, now I had, in a sense, given up my quest. I didn't want to win whatever pointless battle I'd undertaken; I really just wanted to get laid. I can remember their names, mostly. Mark, music producer. First uncircumcised penis, which, to be honest, horrified me. All I could think was: sea cucumber. I wept *the whole time* we fucked, though I'm pretty sure that was not connected to the uncircumcised penis—just plain maudlin drunkenness. John, high-school boyfriend. The morning after we slept together, he staple-gunned flowers all over my front door but I wouldn't see him again either, for years in fact. A very cute famous singer passing through town with his band, but he doesn't count because I blacked out on top of him, for added squalor, before we could even really get going. And many more, the most representative of whom is, for some reason, Malcolm. We went to dinner and he spent the whole meal telling me he was working on a screenplay of *The Catcher in the Rye;* he was confident he'd have full backing from J. D. Salinger. Yech, I thought (rightly). But I fucked him anyway. I remember him moving on me too gently; I floated away from my body (I was very drunk) and from the ceiling I imprecated, "Do it harder, Malcolm," but he did not. His inability to hear my ghost made me incredibly sad. I left him sleeping like a baby in his bed. A couple of weeks later I came home to find a very long letter from him nailed—à la Martin Luther's theses—to my front door: all that was wrong with me. Like I didn't know already.

Sleeping with strangers became part of this tight world I'd made. It was springtime and I was like a forced narcissus, forcing my own transformation into someone who could live for something besides love—what Josephine might've become if Fitzgerald had let her get up off the couch. There was the sweet dairy smell of melting butter, and the hissing of cassettes, and the needle hanging in the center of my room, and the ridiculous, arrogant curlicues of Derrida's prose. Somehow these things were absolute in a way I liked, unforgiving in the same way as leaving a boy's bed in the middle of the night, just getting up, walking out the door, and riding my bike home through the quiet Seattle streets. I missed the old intensity of love, and it took all this—the butter, the noise, the fucking, the impenetrable philosophy—to make up for it. It was working, though. It was all worth it.

One night a band came over to eat dinner after a show. The guitarist and I had a funny rapport, the kind of rapport that turns into you-know-what. The L-word. Usually I didn't let boys come over to my house; usually I went to theirs. I immediately saw I had made a mistake this time. I was a great one for strewing my clothes on the floor and they stepped all over my undies in their boots. They thumbed through my books and flipped over my postcards and read the sweet, witty messages from faraway friends. They lay down on my bed, rumpling my great-grandmother's patchwork quilt. They demanded food and drink. I made them polenta (natch) and gave them some champagne I happened to have in the fridge. Then I sent them on their way, ruefully holding the hand of the guitarist as he slipped out the door. Goodbye, I said. When they'd gone I put on a Descendents cassette and laid down on the bed and drank champagne from a mug and ate another bowl of polenta. There was no room for love in this house.

"Sometimes life is a thing of determination," I wrote in my diary that first winter when I returned to school. "And when you are determined, you are free." Too right, mate. I looked like a bigger fuckup than ever: the heavy blackout drinking, the promiscuity, the mad butter eating. But my life had become a thing of determination, and so it came to pass that I finally escaped the terrible surrender of will that marked my adolescence. I was no longer ruled by boys but by myself.

Okay, fine, eventually I got a boyfriend, like always. But somehow it didn't crush me; I wasn't subsumed by it. He became part of my student life; I didn't give the whole thing up for him. This time it was the ridiculous Ed, genius artist, punk legend, haver of the coolest friends in Seattle—it was this latter part that really sold me. They were the first group of people I'd ever encountered in my entire life that I wanted to join. Like Josephine, I'd always been "an egotist who played not for popularity but for individual men." But this group was different. Mean and sweet. I wanted to be one of them more than I wanted anything. I had finally admitted that for me there was no arena other than Seattle.

I was especially interested in Ed's friend Victoria, a painter who also owned an art gallery downtown, even though she was only twenty-five. Victoria was six feet tall and beautiful. She loved Patti Smith and seemed to have taken on some of her hero's severe elegance, like style was a library you could check stuff out of. Her legs, clad in their inevitable black tights, were so long that she never quite seemed to have the right place to put them. I knew for a fact that at least three people thought she was their best friend.

Victoria had a tall, handsome, hilariously funny boyfriend, Dave, who was her perfect equal. I adored him, with a little sister's hero worship. At a loud party one night in 1990 in a dank rental house, the four of us—me, Ed, Vic, and Dave—sat drinking in a breakfast nook. It was an old house from the 1910s, so the nook was tiny, while we were all fairly huge. On one side of the table Ed and Victoria sat gossiping. On the other side, wedged onto the tiny bench, I was subjecting Dave to an extravagant flirtation. Somehow we had started talking about power tools—not in a dirty way, just in a silly way—and we were laughing about drills and table saws until we couldn't get our breath, leaning into each other and egging each other on. Finally, Dave got up to get more beer. Victoria, sweet Vic, always a sport, always ready with a laugh, always the nicest person in the room, looked at me with a smile on her face and said, "Why don't you sit next to your *own* boyfriend?" I moved next to Ed and was uncharacteristically silent for the rest of the evening.

That night as I fell asleep I thought about Victoria. "Thought" is a strong word. What I did was, I felt. It was rare for a friend to make me feel. And what I felt was that I wanted her friendship. A strong wanting. The kind of wanting I usually reserved for sex and love. Now it was coming, bam, in the middle of the night and with that forcefulness I knew all too well, but it was about a new thing, about this friend. I wanted to change my life, to be worthy of her. Also, I wanted to be a Hegelian because that was the smartest thing I could think of. That would be the new me: Hegelian and friend of Vic. That was all I wanted. But how to go about it? The Hegel part was easy; just read some Hegel. Okay, not that easy. The Vic part I was going to have to work at.

I stopped speaking to Dave altogether. Sometimes I think that moment she said "Why don't you sit next to your *own* boyfriend" was the most important moment in my entire life; not just because it led to the most important friendship I will ever have but because she explained so succinctly how to be a friend. How to stop living for boys.

I mounted a charm offensive and eventually wore her down—several months later we went on our first friend date. She picked me up in her Impala and drove me to see *Thelma and Louise* at the Guild 45th in Wallingford. I thought Brad Pitt was kinda hot; she wasn't so sure. At the time, we didn't see our destiny in those two ladies—who seemed old to us—driving off into the sunset together.

<u>July 1, 1989, age twenty-two</u>

Completely allied with masculinity—that unbelievably beautiful feeling of "I shouldn't be here, I'm here" that I get whenever I am around some testosterone.

16

How to Be in Seattle in the '90s

Have puffy hair. Wear very large clothes. Later, when you look back at photos of the '90s, you will think, *So much fabric.*

Go to Septieme on Second Avenue in Belltown and sit in the courtyard and salt the butter, which is served French and unsalted and exotic.

Have a job that pays just enough for rent and beer. Some (good) (bad) months, rent probably costs you less than beer.

Drink a lot. Drink at the Comet. If you don't know where to go or what to do, go to the Comet and drink. It's a cliché for a reason. If you're on your own and don't see anyone you know, chat with Jason behind the bar, or Mike. Get a weird rash from resting your forearms on the Comet's splintered bar. Name this rash Bar Burn.

Say to your best friend, "It's a good thing we're not alcoholics so we can get drunk every night!"

Ride your bike home down Fairview, with its long swooping curves. Think drunkenly how Fairview is like the Renton S-curves of the city.

Sunbathe topless at Denny Blaine. Glare righteously at the cops who come to ogle.

Go to shows. Go like it's your job. Go to the Off Ramp and the Vogue and the OK Hotel and RKCNDY and the Storeroom and the Central and the Crocodile and the Ditto. (Don't go to the Weathered Wall, ever.) Go to so many shows that you get bored of it. Go to so many shows that seeing the Screaming Trees one more time sounds like a chore. You will never tire of seeing Flop, however.

End up at the Dog House.

Save your extra money to buy books at Bailey/Coy. Books of impenetrable theory, which will sit unread on your shelf.

When you visit other cities, get asked about Seattle. The people you meet want to move there. No one used to move to Seattle except aeronautical engineers and, like, rabid fishing enthusiasts. No one used to know where Seattle even *was*. They thought maybe it was in Oregon.

When you fly home from visiting friends in Chicago, see a young man at O'Hare headed for your gate. He has long hair and a leather jacket and a battered guitar case. Feel obscurely sad about this. Don't tell him that Seattle has become a place he wants to go precisely because no one ever went there. No one was looking, and a bunch of music and other stuff got made. Don't tell him he's going to ruin it simply by going there. Be afraid it's true, though.

Wish that you could write. Feel amazed by the girls around you, including your best friend, who are making art and starting bands and opening bars—Seattle looks like a boys' club, but there're these girls all around you making shit.

Crash your boyfriend's poker party. Smoke a cigar. Feel daring.

Try to read *Infinite Jest*. Fail.

Notice that more people are talking more freely about heroin. It's always been around, but suddenly it seems to be scouring the town. Hear about overdoses. Quit taking drugs.

Watch people quit their bands.

Lament the closing of the Dog House. Somehow related: Think about how it's maybe time to get a real job.

Start to write. Write about food and art and film and books. Feel a little embarrassed about it, and exposed. You were good at being a rock chick. This is so . . . nerdly. Keep going. Suspect that everything good in life might actually be nerdly.

Always think of the new Septieme as the new Septieme.

Watch your best friend lose one art studio after another. She's evicted from buildings in Westlake, South Lake Union, downtown, and Ballard. Everything is coming down so everything else can go up. This will continue for decades—she will eventually become an internationally recognized artist but will never find a Seattle studio that is safe from developers.

Books start to come out about bands you know. Read them and feel weirded out. Talk to some people who are starting a museum—a museum of the music you grew up with. Watch the messy drunken unhinged nights of your city, disjointed and pointless, turn into a story. The story is both wrong and right. Resolve to keep writing.

Move to Phinney Ridge because it's cheap and you can have a yard.

Watch a lot of people get a lot of money, quickly. Wonder *Why them?*

Eat the banana cake at Longshoreman's Daughter as often as possible.

Meet your husband at the alternative newspaper where you work. Become friends with him because he's the first boy you've ever known who's serious about writing. Also, he's incredibly cute: tall and dark, with long eyelashes that lie across his cheeks as extravagantly as if he were Mimi in *La Bohème*. Feel an almost immediate deep tender sweetness toward him, and also a sense of inevitability. Be pleased when he listens to you and when he laughs at your jokes. Experience an incredible yearning the first time he nuzzles your cheek. Think, *I want this.*

Get married, standing on the shore of Agate Passage in the drizzle on a gray October day. Have the Hank Williams All-Star Tribute play the reception; ask them to do "Someone to Watch Over Me" for your first dance with your husband. Have a baby. Be muzzy from lack of sleep. Feel unsure about where you belong in the city. You are a writer now, and so's your husband, and as such, perpetually short on dough. Breastfeed your baby (you breastfeed, of course—you're not a monster) and muse about what you will do. Your beloved native city, so content with—even proud of—its loserdom, has become a city of winners.

Cover your baby's head with kisses. You don't know it now, but one day when she's a teenager she will say to you "Your past is our history," and you will feel an indescribable excitement and satisfaction.

December 3, 1981, age fourteen

I'm glad Amy and I are friends again. It feels really good. There's nothing better than having good girl friends. Chrissy says Sam told her he likes me. Mark is cool but he's soooo short. I dislike Arthur Fiedler. He was a jerk. He looked so jolly, but I'm sorry, no. He hated little kids.

17

Dante and Virgil in L.A.

Hell's Gate, River Acheron, 2012

When I turned forty-five, Vic and I began a phase of going to Los Angeles fairly often—every year or so. She got interested in the art scene there; I, you know, went along. You must understand that in Seattle, L.A. is considered just . . . wrong. The place everything bad flows out of. If you look the way I look (like a tragic old hippie) and you grow a lot of kale and are preoccupied with the vicissitudes of motherhood, you are not supposed to like L.A. But I did and so did Vic. We loved seeing the ocean of course, but we were just as drawn to the Los Angeles River as we were to the glamorous Pacific; the river flowed through Culver City, our neighborhood of choice; we liked its tragic history. Because we often shared a brain, the river reminded Vic of *Chinatown* on my behalf and that gave me a chance to think about Roman Polanski, as was my surprising new habit.

These were kamikaze trips; we didn't really have the dough or the time to be gallivanting around like this. We went for a night or two, stayed somewhere on the cheap. The fact that we could ill afford these trips should serve only to underline how much we needed them. Or how much we needed something; L.A. was a stand-in for all our longing.

1. Limbo

We were walking down the bare brown slope of Baldwin Hill, a hill where we walked pretty often but whose name we could never remember, so we insisted upon calling it Bernal Heights (the name of another bare brown hill, this one in San Francisco), which made us laugh at our own dottiness. The hill overlooked the gray gutter of the Los Angeles River. I had been trying to write about being young and finding it painfully difficult. I was tormented by the question of identity in a way I never had been before. It confused me, the way reading coming-of-age memoirs often confused me. A problem of narration. Who was telling the story of young Claire? Asking this question made me feel like I was floating in space. I thought about Geoff Dyer's writing, and the way he often situates himself in the present day before he engages in nostalgia or memory.

"It's like he's in a room, writing, and he tells you about the room, and once that's established, then you go with him wherever he takes you into the past, and you're willing to go there with him because you know where he's writing *from.* It all makes sense because of that."

"So write about the room. Write about where you are now."

"Bernal Heights?"

"Yeah!" We collapsed in giggles. For a second we couldn't remember *where* we were. Maybe we were nowhere.

2. The Lustful

We took turns driving, so each of us got a chance to be the passenger. Unlike real Angelenos, we absolutely loved driving around town, from Culver City to Santa Monica, from West Hollywood to Silver Lake. We listened to two songs: "I Love L.A." by Randy Newman and "Los Angeles" by X. Sometimes we added in the Minutemen's "History Lesson—Part II" for the part where he says "Drove up from Pedro / We were fucking corndogs."

I tried to sneak in "Estimated Prophet" from *Terrapin Station* by the Grateful Dead, with its chorus of "California, I'll be knocking on the golden door," and Vic threw a fit as we barreled down Sepulveda. "Get that shit OFF!" She's always had better taste than I do, I admit it freely.

I checked my phone when Vic drove. I was still e-mailing with the Californian short-story writer, the one who gave me the disruptive kiss. All we did was tell each other jokes and trash whatever book we happened to be reading for the other person's amusement. But still: *we*. That wasn't right. Not that he was the only one—there seemed to be a number of distractions. I wanted to be taken out of myself and almost anyone would do.

3. The Gluttonous

What is the point, neither of us asked.

We wandered around Culver City, looking at restaurants jammed with the young, until we finally decided on a cool-enough restaurant called Akasha, where they clearly clocked us as a lesbian couple and gave us the royal treatment. We got this a lot. They found us a nice booth and an ice bucket for our wine and asked if it was a special occasion "for the two of you." Yes! we said, because it was. Even to this day, we can make each other laugh by saying "ice bucket." We drank two bottles of Grüner Veltliner and ate something interesting: a salad with expensive cheese in it; a fish cooked in a way one can't cook fish at home. We talked about people in our fields we were mad at—that is, people in our fields who were more successful than we were. This made us giddy and hilarious. A ridiculous jazz combo played in the corner.

We picked up a bottle of vodka at the Trader Joe's on the corner and shambled back to our room, where we lay on the bed together drinking. I began to drill Vic about a sexual encounter she'd had many decades ago. I'd never heard the whole story and I demanded that she tell me everything. I promised her I wouldn't tease her about it if she told me. I nagged and nagged and finally she told me. I immediately began to tease her mercilessly about it. We fell asleep mid-sentence. I was so drunk that I chased her across the bed, crowding her until, in the early hours of the morning, she fell out. The thunk she made woke me up and I found her sitting on the floor, rubbing her head in confusion like a cartoon character.

4. The Avaricious and the Prodigal

Victoria and I were staying in a friend's Culver City mother-in-law apartment, which sat behind their groovy modernist house where they stowed their two groovy towheaded daughters. The daughters were like part of the design: They twirled through empty spaces in pink tutus. The cool world had passed me by, as a mother. When I was a young mother, the cool thing was to have an old house filled with old shit. Now you were supposed to have a modern house with great slabs of cement for the children to clonk their heads on. The houses were like very plain platters on which the children's beauty was served up. There were new rules I didn't understand, ways people wrapped their babies and fed them and presented them to the world. New expressions of upper-middle-class awareness. And I was past it, and my children were at home, with my brilliant sweet kind husband, who maybe was having his own doubts and yearnings but I wasn't thinking about that, and I was here, in this tiny Culver City apartment.

5. The Wrathful and the Sullen

I was on my own this trip, Victoria-less, here for work and staying at the Standard, known to an L.A. friend as the Ty-D-Bol Hotel for the sky-blue neon of its exterior. When I walked into the lobby, I encountered a lot more blue and also a sexy lady napping inside a little vitrine-like chamber behind the check-in desk. I became ensorcelled by her, and stood and stared for a moment, until I realized that's not how it's done and checked in and then headed for the bar by the pool, where I was to meet a writer friend. The bar, the pool, the sky—all matched the lobby, white and blue, though somehow subtly grubby. One sensed a certain ambient quality of HPV.

I put a damper on the scene at the bar simply by showing up. The sun streamed across the pool to the little table where I nursed my martini and looked lonesome, even though I was not especially. Middle-aged women in bars always look lonesome. I was discovering that there's really no dignified way to go to seed as a woman. Even if you feel happy, full to the brim with that mysterious interior majesty that can sometimes come with drinking alone, you don't look replete. You look like a saddo. When I was young, a boy once fell in love with me because, he said, I "looked sad." He found my visible sadness moving, sexually, romantically. That's not the kind of sad I looked now.

There was nothing mysterious or alluring or Jeanne Moreau–like about my sadness. I, with my sadness, was lowering the tone. I was a wet blanket on a hot bed. My friend arrived and I forgot all about it in a flurry of another-martini-ordering and hugs. As night fell, we wrapped ourselves like *nonnas* in giant scarves; the sky was a beautiful, non-Ty-D-Bol light blue and reminded us of nature, even as the terrible muffled sounds of Sunset Strip hummed away.

6. The Heretics

There was something about galleries and museums in L.A. that was just right. All that bleached white space mimicking the air of L.A., which was, to me, as much white as it was blue. Also: A gallery was an idealized space; California was an idealized space. Perfect places in the mind. And of course a gallery was like California in that they were both image containers.

In the winter when I was forty-six, we went to L.A. on a kind of art-seeing blitz. We visited maybe a dozen or more galleries in two days. What I was after was the bright white light and the feeling of possibility, both of which had faded from my life. I'd spent the drizzly autumn in my shed remembering and writing about being a sad girl. My husband had mostly been away for work, and who could blame him. I'd been pulled through my days by my children, by those terrible beautiful funny e-mails, which just kept coming, and by a book Vic told me to read, with the most awesomely pretentious title of all time: *Seeing Is Forgetting the Name of the Thing One Sees,* Lawrence Weschler's life of his close friend, the quintessentially Californian artist Robert Irwin, based on decades of conversation between the two. Vic wanted me to read it to understand her thoughts about perception—Irwin apparently could barely be bothered

to make a mark on canvas, or at least that was how his paintings looked to me: creamy squares crisscrossed by a precise yellow line or two. There were not very many of these paintings
extant—even though they looked like so little trouble to make,
it turned out they were quite . . . rigorous? I don't know. I liked
the parts of the book where he bet on the ponies.

And now it was time! We were at the Hammer Museum
to see one, a real Robert Irwin painting, and Victoria was all
aflutter. We'd just had coffee at the place we called the Tobey
Maguire coffee shop because we saw him there once. We were
both in a happy cheerful mood for a change. There is the way
that women friends are supposed to be when they go on a "girls
weekend" together—fizzy, indulgent—and we were that way
right now, though usually we fell short of the mark. We arrived
at the wall and there it was and it looked to me like decor in
someone's parents very groovy and expensive living room in
1982 but I didn't utter that out loud. I could see there was something more interesting going on, but I had no idea what it was.
The book was no help at all—except as a document of a friendship. A friendship between a critical, skeptical writer and an artist who believed in the abstract and had the generosity of spirit
to attempt to articulate how and why.

7. The Violent (Against the Self;
Against Property; Against Others)

Vic moved to L.A. for a couple of months. The expense, the
inconvenience—this was all a measurement of her desperation
and her seriousness. She didn't know what else to do; she felt, in
every way, at a loss. I often felt that my own lostness, my sense
of constraint, my yearning, had to do with being a mom, being
in a state of what I saw as extreme domesticity. But Vic—whose
life was considerably more glamorous, more carefree than my

own—felt it too. If she, with her parties and her rock shows and her artist friends and her long sojourns to foreign countries, felt trapped, well what was to become of me? We knew we were ingrates, we talked about it all the time, but the sadness crowded us all the same. We were like Luke and Leia in that scene from (the real) *Star Wars,* when the walls are closing in on them. We refused to call it menopause. First of all, it *wasn't* that, yet, and second of all, the very term annoyed us. When men have existential crises—when Richard Ford, for instance, limns the male at midlife—it doesn't get called by some dumb hormonal name. It's a "universal human experience." We were having those, "universal human experiences," not menopause, or so we kept telling ourselves. Women can, after all, see the same thing on the horizon that men see.

Vic got a studio for painting and a little apartment for sleeping and was howlingly lonesome. Even her work was changing. For years and years her paintings and drawings, while abstract, were exhaustively figured and detailed, an exterior expression of her interior whirring: repeated obsessive marks. This work was beautiful and *very* popular. People loved that shit. For the viewer, it was a relief to look at these hundreds or thousands of tiny marks that together made a huge and beautiful shape, a relief to see our own neuroses, our own obsessiveness, so clearly expressed and turned into something beautiful. But now she just wanted to make plain shapes, the plainer the better. It was not what the people wanted. But it was what she wanted to do.

I went to visit her and we walked the beach from Venice to Santa Monica and back again, though we might as well have just stayed in one place, because what was the point. We might as well have been Beckett's Winnie, buried up to our necks in the California sand. This move, this walk, everything we did, was a disruption, an injury against the order of things, which was inertia, entropy, my bed. The light was supposed to make us feel better but felt faded and wavering. Like us!

My visit was short; I needed to get home and mind the kids and earn some dough. Bruce had to go away for another work trip. Someone had to earn the money, or so he told me. All this mooning thinking about olden dayz of yore wasn't helping our family budget. *Sell a book,* he said. *I'm going as fast as I can,* I said. Which admittedly wasn't very fast. He didn't care what else I did, didn't mind my travel and my mopeyness, as long as I started making some serious coin. He couldn't take much more of being left holding the bag, financially speaking. My spiral into despair was taking him down with me, but I didn't know how to stop the fall.

8. Fraud

No matter the season, we went to the Getty. We looked at whatever art they had lyin' around, but we were really there to see the garden, designed by our withholding boyfriend Robert Irwin. We liked it in every season, but maybe best in fallow January. There was something lovely about the bare rosebushes set in their concentric circles around the fountain; the twigs and sticks that surely would bud soon. In winter, minus the obscuring green, the garden was laid bare in its intentionality.

We were feeling pretty fallow ourselves. We walked under the bare trellises, looked down at the white light of the city below, kicked rocks, talked about work. Neither of us seemed to be able to work. Maybe we were just worn out. We'd been doing this a long time. It was sort of funny. Ha. All around me, on my island and in the fancier neighborhoods of Seattle, the moms were returning to painting and writing with renewed zeal, rediscovering their creativity, searching out their groove in their forties. Meanwhile Vic and I, we were *pooped.* Done. The newly creative moms seemed to come in droves, yearning and rich, and they had new paints and new cars, children with brushed hair and husbands with jobs. But we had something they wanted, this thing we had been growing throughout our adult lives, like mushrooms in the basement. It had sometimes seemed dark and shameful, sometimes prideful, this work we'd been doing, but here they all came. They were rushing, and we, meanwhile, we were wilting. We were worn out from the dodgy finances, the way our work ate our time—couldn't you always be working more? We had exhausted the bohemian life, found the hard graft at its core.

Vic, for instance, had been working for years on a pair of crossed brass sticks. She was obsessed with the pure abstraction of the project. This was sort of cool to think about, but not exactly practical. She was, in fact, going broke as she kept crossing and recrossing brass rods, trying out new gauges, figuring out how to hang such a thing. Meanwhile, I continued writing reams of pages about the sad girl I had been, writing that would never see the light of day, and yet I couldn't stop. All of this was taking a lot of time, time we could've spent making work that would, you know, sell. Our crisis held us in thrall and was starting to make us go broke, a little.

As we wandered through Irwin's abstract Versailles, we talked about wire gauge. She had bags under her eyes. Would this brass X ever even eXist? Neither of us had any idea. We couldn't help it, we really were like Beckett's Winnie, whom one critic called a "hopeful futilitarian." We were wondering if we even knew how do to our jobs, or if they were even jobs at all. We felt like giant frauds. We were sure things would get better pretty soon, and yet—probably not for a long time.

9. Treachery

I should've been at home, and I wasn't.

November 19, 1989, age twenty-two

Don DeLillo's most photographed barn in America: sometimes
(always) I feel over-perceived like that.

18.

Three Kisses, in the Passive Voice

1.

I was invited to the party and was taken there. I was given a large bourbon. In the midst of the loudness and the smoking and the gossip, I was swept up in conversation with a musician I admired. A little grubby, always good in my book. I was flirted with by said musician. I was urged to leave the party, to go get a drink at a bar. I was led to his car. ("Never go with a hippie to a second location."—Jack Donaghy.) I was installed in the passenger seat—oh, the passenger seat. I was driven. I was taken to a dive bar. I was asked questions: Did I like being a writer? Did I like being married? Did I like life on my uncool nerdy bourgeois [not his exact phrasing] island? My jokes were laughed at. And then my leg was touched, and my hand was taken.

The syntax begins to feel tortuous. One can't abdicate responsibility for a sustained period of time. Even the language is against us.

I was pulled outside, and kissed. It happened to me. I was deliciously mauled, on a side street in a busy neighborhood on a cloudy, invisible-mooned Seattle night. It happened to me.

.   .   .

A sadist, a masochist, a pedophile, a zoophile, and a pyromaniac are all sitting around a jail cell.

"I know what," says the zoophile. "Let's fuck a cat."

"Even better: a kitten," says the pedophile.

"Let's beat it up and then fuck it," says the sadist.

"Let's find a kitten, beat it up, fuck it, and set it on fire," says the pyromaniac.

There's a long pause. "Meow," says the masochist.

I wanted something—I wasn't sure what—to happen to me. In this way I was like so many girls and women in literature: Emma Bovary, duh, but also Chekhov's three sisters, and the bored cousins in Nancy Mitford's *Pursuit of Love,* and Kitty and Lydia Bennet, who were a two-girl *machine* for making things happen to them. But getting someone to do something to you is harder than it might seem. Meow. I wasn't quite a masochist, but I had the masochist's unique frustration: I kept having to make shit happen, when I wanted shit to *happen to me.* The fact is: This kiss did not happen in the passive voice. It happened in the active voice, if my Magoo-like fumbling can be thought of as active. I laid the groundwork, perhaps not even consciously. I put myself in this person's path and surprised him with sudden bursts of intimacy and rude jokes—that is, my own neolithic brand of flirting. I essentially groomed him to dominate me. So then I could slip into passive voice, surreptitiously keeping an eye on things, actively making sure they were moving along toward the fullest expression of my passivity. Which would be some form of penetration: in this case, his tongue in my mouth. Penetration, just like Helena Bonham Carter got in *A Room with a View.* And it was good. A strange tongue, a strange biceps. A strange force. "I'll miss the 12:15 ferry if I don't go now," I said. Saved by my safe island once again. Nothing would ever happen to me *there*.

2.

The party was in a dozy subdivision. I went to be nice. The hostess was a woman I liked; we were hovering on the doorstep between acquaintanceship and friendship. The party was typical of my safe island: a lot of voluble, smart, still-beautiful women chatting and cackling away; a few softer-spoken bearded men interspersed. I sat quiet—unusual for me—and listened to someone talk about her divorce; there had been a crop of them that year, like rhubarb. My friend Melinda came in, looking glamorous, the way a fresh divorce takes some women. She looked thinner and somehow more big-boobed. She had that crazed gleam in her eye I had come to recognize. Maybe I had it too. She strode up to me and kissed me on the mouth. "Woman!" she said. "You look HOT." And she kissed me on the mouth again. *Avec* tongue. She slipped me the sashimi.

I drank a lot of bourbon (a theme! a motif!) and got in a terrible circular argument with a woman who thought authors should spend more time thinking about what readers want. As someone who has spent almost all my time thinking about nothing but what readers want for more than twenty years, I couldn't see how I could possibly do it any more than I already was, but she was *very* angry. She was also drinking bourbon. I was now flat-out drunk.

With my last shred of sense I rose from the couch and left the room, ostensibly to go to the bathroom but really to gather my shit and go home. Nothing good would follow from here. In the foyer, Melinda stopped me and reinserted her tongue in my mouth. We slipped outside, giggling. And the next thing I knew, I was pushed up—passive voice—against the garage door. While the people inside drank wine and discussed their children's summer camp plans, we had at each other.

It was as if the event rose up from somewhere deep in my perverse subconscious. Not perverted, or not just that, but perverse, in the sense of Edgar Allan Poe's "Imp of the Perverse": Poe is talking in that story about the part of a person—the part of *me*—that wants to do wrong just because there is wrong to be done. The part of me that craves normalcy and security and then wants to disrupt it. The part that wants to *épater* the fuck out of the bourgeoisie, but still wants to be one of them. The part of me that lives on the safe pretty island and wants to set fire to it.

The thing was, it didn't do the trick. Who cared if some girl wanted me? Girls are pretty, girls are hot, but ultimately, in a sexual encounter, girliness needed to inhere only *in me*.

I went home and fell into bed with my husband. Told him what had happened. He nuzzled me, unflustered. Two chicks together, that's cool, he didn't say. He slid his hands around on me. Is it a problem, I asked. A little tipsily. The real problem was that I drove home from the party. Careening down those pretty roads in my Prius, wild-eyed, radio on. My bad shameful decisions were stacking up. Pick one, use it as kindling. All around me good people were sleeping in nice farmhouses. Maybe a house with a plum tree and a *major* vegetable garden and a tastefully chaotic kitchen, whose fridge is filled with the umami-rich foods of the overeducated and open-minded: hard rocks of parm, fish sauce, bone broth, grass-green olives the size of quail eggs. The kind of house I dreamed of when I got married, when I first had children. These good houses, sheltering these considered lives, do they hold people as dopey and hard-headed and sinful as me? Bruce was moved by the idea of what I'd been up to, and rolled on top of me.

3.

This was supposed to be fun. It had been fun, up until now. Bruce was reporting a story on the Louisiana three-strikes law, and I had come along to help. We stayed with friends at a beautiful house in the Garden District. That afternoon, Bruce and I had hung out at the New Orleans courthouse, laughing that we were reenacting *Hart to Hart,* the terrible early-'80s TV show about a crime-solving couple living the high life. We ate oyster po'boys for lunch and then went out for drinks at Napoleon House. I chatted too much with the person on the stool next to me, Bruce grew irritated, I called him a stick and picked a fight with him. At moments like these I became irrationally enraged. Our argument went:

"You want me to be Ed," said Bruce, referring to my good-time Charlie ex-boyfriend.

"No, I just want you to lighten up."

"I'm lightening up fine. You're just too critical."

What I didn't or couldn't say was what every stereotypical middle-aged man doesn't or can't say to his wife: I want you to be a stranger. I want you to be strange. I want you, and at the same time I want my life to change, and I want that change to happen *to me.*

That was our argument: the one that actually occurred, and also the one that didn't. Now it was raining, hard. Not Seattle rain, more like water-from-a-bucket rain. And colder than it was supposed to be. I had my pashmina pulled up over my head like a Greek peasant lady. Honestly, I was old enough to be one. The thin wool was soaked through. Bruce walked grimly next to me, looking extra tall on the old sidewalk, I have no idea why. He took my hand. I was crying.

We stopped walking. We ducked under the awning overhanging a bar. Inside, patrons were propped up on stools, backs curved in a universal slump that said "I'm here for the night." I envied them their commitment to unsobriety. I was here with an upright husband, who counted drinks. I looked regretfully at the drinkers, all men except one middle-aged (my age, as I had to remind myself) woman with long unnaturally dark unnaturally flat hair, which didn't so much flow down her back as rest there, like an old pet. I thought again: There is no way for a middle-aged woman to seek oblivion gracefully. I wanted to press my cheek against the window to feel its coolness.

"It must suck to be you," he said.

"Wait, what?" I said. A thing my twelve-year-old son and his friends said.

"Every time we fight I can see you going down the road to divorce. I can see you weighing it in your mind. It's all over your face."

"I do? I guess I do. Don't you?"

"No, because I didn't have your weird childhood."

"Well, I mean, divorce *is* an option."

"It's not supposed to be an option *all the time*." The ozonic muffled drumming of the rain on the awning overhead. "Sometimes you're just supposed to be married."

"I can't help it. I never feel like it's a done deal."

"Okay, if it's not a done deal, how about this? How about we separate?"

The beignet sat leaden in my stomach. I thought, perhaps not entirely illogically, of dinner parties I would not be invited to as a single woman. The expense of a setting up a second household. Changing the batteries in the smoke alarm. The empty bed. All that old business. At the same time, I felt lighter. When I was in Indonesia many years ago a parrot landed on my head. Everyone oohed and aahed and told me how lucky I was, but all I could feel was its weight, surprisingly heavy. Bruce's words felt like the moment the parrot took off from my head.

I am a touchy person, a hand holder, a slinger of arms across shoulders, at least when it comes to my gangly husband. But I hadn't touched him all evening, or maybe for days. Now I leaned into him. My scarf smelled like wet poodle. I kissed his beautiful mouth so firmly that our lips made a cartoon sound: Smack!

Bruce was giving me a choice. He was refusing to let me drift along, passively being married, passively being discontented. I would have to *choose*. It wasn't enough just to be wanted, I would have to want as well, if I was to stay married.

"Let's shove off," I said. "We don't want to be late for our dinner reservation."

I was pulled into the rain and then we were both soaked in objective correlative. I was walked away from the lonelies and the drunks, the people who would never be solved. I was half saddened to be taken away from those people. But: reservations, and Bruce's hunger.

May 7, 1982, age fifteen

I hate the fucking boys in our class. They're such assholes!
They classify all girls in our class who are even a little pretty
as class-skipping sluts. What fuckers!

19

Don't Tell Anyone

It is my blessing and my curse to professionalize every single enthusiasm that floats through my distractible head. It's this way for many journalists—you become fascinated by a subject, and then you kill the thing you love by turning it into your job. I have been a food critic, a visual-art critic, a film critic, and for many years a book critic. I was an expert on none of these things but an enthusiastic consumer of them. I'd written an entire book about my favorite hobby, yoga. (And I *still* like it, against all the oddsmakers' predictions.)

It was probably inevitable that I would write something about sex. My re-preoccupation dragged on for another year; it felt like it was taking over my life. I wondered what the hell was going on—was everyone gripped by these thoughts? I wanted to write about it, but I didn't want to confess exactly what I was going through, which seemed embarrassing, and what would my in-laws think?

So what I did was this: I wrote a book review about fucking. My piece was a long portmanteau review that looked at a bunch of memoirs by women about sex, and found—surprise!—that the best ones were complicated, thoughtful, doubtful, confused.

I also discovered an interesting problem for a woman writer of a sex memoir: It always seems like an attempt to incite desire in the reader.

This book review, once published, brought an unforeseen gift, or burden: Suddenly everyone wanted to tell me about his or her sex life. I mean everyone. I heard secrets, nonstop, for months. I had thought I was alone, but all across the land, it seemed, there were people suffering a middle-aged anomie that found its expression through some kind of sexual travail. Everyone was either having an affair, or couldn't get their spouse to sleep with them, or both. According to my findings, half the world seemed to want it all the time, and half the world seemed to want it not at all, and these two halves were mostly married to each other. You'd think this might be a gender division, but you'd be wrong.

Secret 1

I was sitting in a café, talking with a very serious novelist, one half of a power couple. She had long, wayward hair, as if her thoughts couldn't be contained by her head, and the kind of sharp, miss-nothing eyes you normally see only in the old, though she was my age. Younger. She was a mother of four. We'd never met before. She was passing through town, read my sex article, wanted to meet.

"Yeah," she said, smiling. "So." She was at a loss for words. I bet that didn't happen to her very often. She slung one booted leg over the other and ran a hand through her hair. She looked like she was about to opine about drilling in the Arctic, or denounce Philip Roth. I waited.

"Um, I keep *going out*," she said. "I mean, when I'm supposed to be home. Like every night. I can't be going out like this.

Dude. I have four kids. Who *all have homework.* And yet . . ." Her eyes looked excited but wary. She wanted to tell me something, but she'd only just met me.

"I go out, as much as I can. I leave my husband at home with the kids and do you know where I go?"

"No," I said.

"I go out to bars. My god, I've barely been to a bar in like fifteen years because I've been a little busy *reproducing*." She humbly, nicely did not add that she'd been busy becoming a great writer, though she'd been doing that too.

"Do you go by yourself?" Perhaps I was leading the witness a teeny tiny bit.

"I go with friends. Man-type people." She re-twined her nervous legs. She paused and gave me a long, knowing look, holding my gaze. Her look contained a certain amount of pain. A certain amount? A lot. "Well, you know," she said.

"A particular man-type person?" I asked.

"Maybe," she said. "I don't want to stop."

Secret 2

A guy I met that winter—for someone who never got out of bed, I seemed to meet a lot of guys that winter—called me up. He was driving across Canada on an ill-conceived book tour.

"Oh, hi!"

"Oh, hi!"

We giggled stupidly.

I didn't really know this person. I'd been helping him with a memoir proposal, ostensibly. I was no longer really any good at male–female friendship and I had zero idea if we were friends, or flirting, or what. But I liked him, and he was a bit ahead of me in his career, and it's good to have people like that in one's life.

"So, I just broke up with my girlfriend."

"I'm sorry?" I said with a question in my voice. You never know.

"Naw, it's okay," he said in his laconic way. "She wouldn't fuck me."

"What? Like, never?"

"Like, never. Like, seasonally. I got my springtime fuck, my summer's fuck. Et cetera."

"That's . . . not so good," I said.

"Yeah, well, last week I was teaching a workshop at"—he named a college—"and I sort of accidentally slept with one of my students. An undergrad."

"Oh. Oops."

"Yeah, oops. Don't tell anyone, okay."

"Okay." Silence, the sound of him driving, Canada rolling past like gorgeous oblivion. "How was it?" I asked eventually. I really wanted to know. Somewhere in the last few months, my native judgmentalism, once an extravagant, robust flower, had wilted or softened into curiosity.

"How *was* it? It was *awesome*. It was sex."

"Oh good!" I said, genuinely happy for him. We started to talk about book proposals and then he had to ring off. "Great article, by the way," he said, as if my sex essay had nothing to do with his confession.

Secret 3

A note from a college friend, via Facebook: "Loved the piece. Struck a chord. These days it seems like I want to Do It all the time and [husband's name redacted] never wants to. I don't know what to do. Am seriously thinking about having an affair but HOW???? How do you even do that?"

Secret 4

Speaking of Facebook, my "Other Messages" folder was chock-full of notes from middle-aged dudes, strangers who read my piece. They sent me song lyrics, poems, links to pieces of music that gave them feelings. They assured me: Women's sexuality is underappreciated! Except by them! Also, would I like some help with it?

Secret 5

I ran into an old friend at a backyard BBQ. He matter-of-factly informed me he was having a midlife crisis and the thought of an affair had crossed his mind. But he was pretty busy. Also, he said, waving his hand comically up and down in front of his aging body, as if to display it, "Who'd *have* us?"

Who indeed. Despite my compatibility with my husband—sexual and otherwise—I too felt a sort of abstract yearning toward an affair, toward strange, but it was hard to imagine who it would be. The young musician? The Californian, who remained where he belonged—in e-mails, in Cali? The man who lived on my island who was sort of funny-looking, but for some reason gave me a near-electric shock whenever he touched me; for instance, when we met and he shook my hand. Who'd *have* me? (Well, Bruce.)

All this talk of affairs caught me by surprise. The mere act of imagining an affair had always seemed to me a thought crime. But other people were thinking about it, talking about it, doing it. Was Bruce?

Secret 6

At another backyard BBQ—in fact the nuptials for a long-term couple of lesbian friends—I met a woman who accused me (quite fairly) of heteronormativity in my article. I conceded the point, but she was off and running on another topic, describing how she just broke up with her partner due to sexual incompatibility. She wouldn't tell me any more than that, so I suppose it didn't really count as a secret, but she woefully kept repeating the phrase "sexual incompatibility."

Secret 7

While I was in the bathroom one morning, Bruce picked up my phone, wanting to make a quick call, and saw a couple of e-mails from the e-mailer. He led me outside and sat me in the grass. He put an arm across my shoulder.

"That guy has been writing you. It sort of hurts my feelings." He paused, figuring out what to say. "People like you, you know, Claire," he said. "They love you."

"I know," I said. Even though I didn't really believe him.

"It's okay to have secrets," he said. "Just be careful."

I cried a little, in a pro forma sort of way, wondering as the tears leaked out: Did *he* have secrets? We had been gone from each other so much, traveling alone. I knew it was dangerous, but I also intuited it was the only way for us to be married right now. We were each giving the other a long lead. I was so mired in my own despair it was hard for me to see that Bruce was undergoing something or other as well. We were sort of trundling along, in our separate orbs, next to each other. I didn't know what to do about it, except hope we were headed in the same general direction. I often had an obscure feeling that I wanted to figure out a different way to be married; it had never before occurred to me that Bruce and I were in the midst of inventing it.

Secret 8

Here I had been going around thinking my friends and acquaintances were living morally upstanding, partnered, educated, organic lives. I thought we were like Tennyson's Ulysses in middle age, "Made weak by time and fate, but strong in will." I thought we were made of stern stuff, stuff that wouldn't give way to the chaos of midlife love and sex. The people I knew seemed, above everything else, too sensible for such nonsense. We were fleece-clad Northwesterners, not perfidious Californians or East Coasters! If we needed thrills and adventures, we found them sensibly: paddleboarding the chilly waters of Puget Sound, clad in impervious wet suits (fun, actually); growing vegetables; playing in a band; binge-watching *Wolf Hall*. But all around me marriages were filled with secrecy and longing and adultery and sex problems. I wrote one article, and a door swung open, and now I saw the hidden world that lay beyond.

I taught memoir to adult students at a literary center in Seattle. My students were by and large sober-seeming achievers, dedicated to their careers and their children. Their midlife splashing out consisted of just this: making time for their long-neglected writing. In fact, I was fascinated by their sobriety. I was their teacher, the person in what can only be called a position of authority, and I was by far the nuttiest person in the room. (Something we never talked about: the weird truth that the nuttiest person was the published memoirist, and what that might mean. Did my all-too-apparent neuroses worry them? Did they really want to get into this racket if they were gonna end up like me? The eternal question: Was looniness a prerequisite for making a career as a writer?)

Mostly women, they came to my class directly from work. They wore serviceable blazers or intelligent sweaters and they knew how to put on the right amount of makeup so their faces said "Woman." We talked about their pasts, because you must in order to teach and learn memoir. As with any group of people attracted to this genre—any group of people, period—strange things had befallen them. They were alive to the outlandishness of their personal histories. But what they didn't have, mostly, was lunacy.

So I was a little surprised when one of them—a smooth-haired thirty-something hospital administrator—pulled me aside after class and offered me a ride to the ferry. No, I liked the walk. So she walked with me, and told me she loved my article.

"See, the thing is," she said, "my husband and I have gotten kind of meh in bed, so I suggested we have another woman join us. I've never done that, and I wanted to try it. We found her on Craigslist." On *Craigslist*? I looked at her blazer, her gold studs, her neat laptop bag. What the hell was going on out there in the world? My feeling that there were dimensions unknown to me increased a thousandfold in the space of a moment.

"So it's been going on for months now. And I think they might be in love." Pause. "And, um, I think I might be in love with her too. I don't know. It's eating me alive. I really don't know what to do." She gazed at me from big, hurt eyes. "What should I do?"

I said the only thing I *could* say, the thing it was my job to say: "Write about it."

June 9, 1997, age thirty

Girls make me hot, but it's more the conception of myself as a girl that makes me really crazy. Denigrated, crawling upon my knees.

20

Uchronia

I'm scheduled to fly out of Seattle at the crack of dawn. It can be difficult to make an early flight from my island, so I stay at the SeaTac DoubleTree the night before. I will need to be well rested the next day; I'm presenting at a conference that afternoon. I get to the DoubleTree around 10 p.m. My grandfather, a fur broker, used to host fur auctions here in the 1970s. As a little girl, I visited the auctions with my dad and uncle and cousins. I would give the others the slip and wander among the men, furriers from all over the world who gathered in the vast dim ballrooms speaking in Italian and German and Japanese accents. They spoke in their Babel and smoked cigarettes and cigars and stroked the mink and beaver and rabbit and fox pelts. I would weave through the crowd, trailing my fingers across the furs, feeling their animal aliveness. The provenance of the pelts was in fact a point of confusion for me. Were the animals shaved? This was what I believed; that the animals were tenderly relieved of their pelts and sent, shivering but still alive, on their way. Somewhere in my small person I knew the real truth, but I ignored it. There were long tables of food, just like the long tables of furs. I would drift past the food tables, pause at the cool silver dish of butter balls, tong a couple into my warm paw, pop them into my mouth. My hobby, my other self: butter. I ate butter right from the stick at home. My father called me the dairy queen. A man with a beard like a pelt leaned down and smoothed my hair like a pelt and said something unintelligible. I stood there, my mouth full of melting butter, and let him. There was no sunlight, no birdsong, no clock. Just rows of tables with animal plenty heaped upon them, and men fingering all the stuff to see what was good.

Now I pull my wheelie across the vast lobby, overwhelmed with a sense memory of long-ago animals and men and butter. I am a grown lady on a business trip, I remind myself. Not a girl. I tread on the lozenge-patterned carpet; it's like walking on very ugly 1970s flowers. The hotel is spread over many buildings. I make my way to my room—down long halls, over skywalks, up one elevator and then down another. It's unnerving to be going *down* an elevator to get to a hotel room. Wrong way. We jerk down a floor, into an eternal yellow hallway. I walk and walk, pulling my suitcase; my arm feels like it's getting pulled off. I pass other travelers; we greet one another variously with humorous mugging or averted eyes. There's something embarrassing about this netherworld where we've found ourselves. The labyrinthine passages of the hotel inspire in me a mood of speculative eroticism. A person could do *anything* here, and it would pass unremarked. It is its own city of adultery. Fur and butter and men. I'm in sort of a lather by the time I get to room A3756D or whatever.

A man slips into the room with me before I can stop him. He gives me a grudging smile. I want to check the time, as if I'm going to punch in, but there's no clock in the room. I guess people travel with their iPhones these days, and here we are out of time. The lights are on, because he has to look at me, knit me back together with his regard, because these days I keep flying apart.

He wants me most of all, and yet not enough. He looks at

me for a long time. I shamefacedly take my clothes off, feeling both unformed and crepey—tough combo. Once he has looked at me and, by doing so, established my lovability, indeed my existence, he begins. He has to do the work but he doesn't mind. The worker is the actor, the driver, and he likes that. My job is to be desired; that's it. The bed has one of those fluffy white duvet covers that hotels favor now; the fluffy white duvet cover tells you your bed is clean. We know better, him and me. We remember the quilted filthy hotel coverlets of yore. We know that any bed we lie down in together will be dirty.

Anyway, it's like this: He holds me down on the fluffy white pretend-clean bed and ties my hands over my head. He beats me. With his hand, and then his belt. He hits my face. My face is in peril. I'm not sure I like any of this, and he knows it. I'm genuinely scared and upset. But if he did only stuff I liked, sweet stuff, then neither of us would know what we need to know: that he is in charge. My passivity is absolute and, at long last, satisfied precisely because I'm uncomfortable with what he is doing to me. I've waited and waited to become absolutely passive, to have my volition truly removed. I sort of hate what he's doing to me, therefore I love what he's doing to me. Once his dominion is established, things are more straightforward: plain old-fashioned fucking, in all my holes, until I can't breathe, can only make a bunch of weird noises from somewhere deep inside.

Now, deep in the bowels of the DoubleTree, I finally lose my sense of direction. I normally know where I am, which way is north, which west, etc. But directions—clear, strong cardinal and subtle ordinal—are gone; there's only what he's doing to me and the strange sounds coming out of my mouth. He does it hard because he can. I'll let him do anything he wants, as long as he wants. He comes—evidence that I have pleased him—but I don't care if I come.

Is that so much to ask? A man of authority; a place of anonymity; a time of urgency; an act of perfect submission. It takes all of that to disguise this truth: I love it and I want it. The perfect act is complete and then he's gone—he slips away into the eternal gloaming of the DoubleTree, its hallways casino-timeless. I still have the buttery chocolate chip cookie they gave me at the front desk when I checked in. I draw a bath in the DoubleTree tub, which is like the platonic ideal of a mid-range hotel bathtub: molded fiberglass surfaces and all the hot water you could ever want. I nibble the cookie in the tub; read my book as I adjust the faucets with my toes; fall asleep naked, legs reddened from hot water; wake up at 4:40 to the wake-up call from the DoubleTree lady, affectless as an angel.

I sleepily dress myself and make my way down the hallways to the elevator. The hallways say, You'll never find your way out, it's the DoubleTree forever for you, bub. Nonetheless, after a few wrong turns I eventually come to the elevator. I ride back up with a wifebeater-clad rent boy and his graying trick. I feel like both of them. Each holds an unlit cigarette between his crooked fingers—they're making the long, law-abiding slog to the faraway outdoors to smoke. We banter, laying the normality of speech like a quilt over what just happened to all of us. When I emerge from the elevator my only thoughts are of family and work: Will I make my flight? Will the kids remember their stuff for their after-school activities? I stop to text my husband and then pull my heavy, book-laden wheelie across the flowered carpet toward the lobby espresso bar. I walk past the ballrooms, remembering nothing.

October 27, 1989, age twenty-two

James S. came over last night. He lay me on my back in the kitchen doorway, my legs around his neck. It was very quiet. I love these objectifying types. "I'm going to kiss you some more." I love being done to, how not modern.

21

On Victimhood

I showed my agent some chapters about my teen sluttishness and she wanted to know: Why? This is what we do in writing workshops and at our desks and when we're editing—we ask each other, or we ask our students, or we preemptively ask ourselves: Why? Why are you like this? What made you this way? So my agent said, I need something explaining why you're like this. Like any writer, I felt resistance. There wasn't *room*, there wasn't *time*, I didn't *know*. The way I am is probably due to chemicals as much as anything—oh, impoverished modernity, with your reflexive explanation for every last feeling: It's chemical.

But my agent wanted an answer, so I did this: I traced my hypersexuality to an incident. It's because Jack Wolf got in the ol' sleeping baggerino in 1980. Of course, the idea that an event can change your life is a bullshit narrative construct. That's not how life works. Except when it does. Life works in all kinds of different ways, sometimes all at once.

The fact is, I didn't think about that incident for years and years—certainly not when I was running around with some boyfriend or other. I forgot it as hard as I could. I misremembered it, when I did remember it. And then it started bubbling up as a kind of shorthand explanation for the Way I Am. When I look at my old journals, the incident is mentioned over and over, though always glancingly, with contempt: "That guy tried to seduce me. He must be fifteen years older than me. YUCK! He fed me some good hash though." I wrote that last sentence in order to make myself look cool, FYI. To whom? To my diary, I guess.

As I revisited this younger self, I wanted the sleeping-bag biz to explain things. I wanted to peg my sexuality to it. But now I see it's a pure narrative device and may be useful as such. Not as an excuse but as a still point in the confusing, shifting narrative of my own sexuality. And so Jack Wolf appears again and again in this book—now for the third time.

If the sleeping-bag thingy—say it: *assault;* say it: *molestation*—makes a mark on my book with more emphasis than it had in my actual life, is that a lie? Or is it, in fact, a marker, pointing out a truth? Because the more I think and write about Jack Wolf, the more I realize: Sex has often, for me, had to do with power and vulnerability, with victims and perpetrators. Did Jack Wolf make me that way? I don't know. But he is an emblem of it, a heraldic animal.

Why choose Jack Wolf as my heraldic animal? Why not choose the boy who gave me my first orgasm? (Thanks!) Or the man who loved to put his tongue in my mouth, or the girl into whose pants I stuck my paw? Or any of one of a largish number of people who actually made me feel good or great? Why not choose *Bruce,* who held me in sexual thrall from the first moment we joined hands, in front of an office building on West Mercer Street on a cool, good-smelling night in the spring of 1996? Instead I choose this person who did something *to* me— the first person to do something *to* me.

Maybe what's at work is a kind of interior slut-shaming—if

I suggest that such a damaging moment was the cause of my sexual activeness, then I disavow any good feelings I might have around my own sexuality.

In other words, victimhood came to shape my own concept of my sexuality. When I sat down to write a memoir of my adolescent sex life, for months I could only write about assaults and molestations. Could only write about Roman Polanski, that cartoon rapist. Could only return over and over to that infernal sleeping bag. I only wanted to tell stories of how sex had *happened to me.* Mary Karr has said that the reason she wrote *Cherry,* her memoir of teenage lust, was that teen *sex* was never written about, just teen victimhood. Now that I've had a whack at it, I can see why—it is easier to write the victimhood. The victimhood was like a vehicle that took me closer to what really interested me, what was obsessing me in middle age as it had done in youth: sex. But if I wrote only about assault and predators, I didn't have to face myself as a sexual person.

What I didn't write, wouldn't write, was the truth: How as a teenager I loved to put my tongue in my boyfriend's mouth; how I loved to smell my wetness—and I seemed always to be wet—on his fingers; how, when we parked at the arboretum, I would climb on him like a crazed monkey, and feel a sense of rightness as I slid myself onto him. So happy, so content to be where I was supposed to be. Sex was a home and a site of purest simplicity. You just were. It pains me to write these words more than any other words in this book: I liked it. It's still so hard to say it. The premise of this book is that I was wild and unhappy as a teen, and my unhappiness stemmed from my sex-crazed nature. But what I really felt was what I feel now: Life was hard, and I didn't know what the hell I was doing, and I was profoundly, near-fatally afraid of failure, and sex was the only thing that made me feel better. *And who doesn't want to feel better?*

So the focus on the predatory older male becomes a feint

away from a hard truth: I wanted it. But it also remains a locus of excitement: The idea of being dominated is, um, of interest to me. I like the idea of being made to do it. I mean, more than like. I dig it. I'm into it. I am far from the first person to cop to this. Indeed, suddenly all the middle-aged laydeez seem to want to be dominated. Generally it gets chalked up to overwork. We make so many decisions, at work and at home, that in bed we yearn to be freed from that duty. Our poor husbands: They've worked so hard at being SNAGs (sensitive New Age guys, as we used to call them in the '80s), worked so hard to empower us and partner us. And now their wives are all fantasizing about having some asshole stranger come along and tie us up. It *does* seem unfair. It's also, let's say it, politically dangerous. Culturally dangerous. Women and political activists have struggled for centuries to erase the rapist's most effective defensive trope: She wanted it. These very words, as I write them, dance in the back of my mind, ghouls waiting to burst into the courtroom as I recount my own violation on the witness stand.

But there's a deeper truth as well: I'm still freaked out (still!) simply by being a woman. I dress butch; I can barely stand to put on a skirt. It makes me feel like I'm in drag. The trappings of womanhood embarrass me utterly. At the same time I'm riven by my outsize sex drive. I hate being a woman, and yet I yearn to be fucked as a woman. I yearn to be dominated by a figure of incontestable authority, who will make me become what I never wanted to be: a woman. I don't know how make myself a woman; you do it for me.

My husband knows how hard this can be, the work of turning me into a woman. When we first wed, he bought me a set of La Perla undies in unimpeachable good taste. I mean, come on, La Perla, that's as fancy as it gets. All I felt was embarrassment, for both of us. The soft pale blue stuff resided in the back of my top dresser drawer for years; I wasn't ready to be that kind of girl. Or any kind of girl. But he is a wily, determined soul, and he figured out other ways to get the job done, the job of turning me into a woman—a job rendered all the more difficult by the fact that I would not speak about what I wanted, but expected him just to know. That was my fantasy: not to have to speak. Because speaking would make it real, would make it *mine*. So he did the work of figuring out what I wanted—his weight on me, his digits in my orifices, his belt around my wrists.

The conflation of victimhood and desire is very hard to talk about, but that doesn't mean it's not real, at least for me. Even writing that sentence makes me afraid, as a feminist, that I am saying something wrong. But for me the freest and purest expression of sex has come with the playacting removal of volition. Being constrained in some manner, whether by hands or ties or just the physical weight of another's body.

Of course the moments—and there are more than I've told here; a list—when I've actually been assaulted were the opposite of pure and free. This is the complication. We all understand that rape isn't really a sexual act. We've been taught it over and over. I remember being told during my second year of college that rape is a continuum, with all violence against women lying somewhere thereon. This was an accepted truth at Oberlin in the 1980s. I think it was issued with your meal punch card. I ran with this idea and soon came to the conclusion that all men are, to some degree, rapists. I can sort of see where my twenty-year-old self was going here. After all, I'd already experienced a typical American woman's share of sexual violence at that point. What I don't quite understand is why I decided to call my gentle, diffident dad that Ohio autumn afternoon and explain this to him, solemnly, twining my fingers in the phone cord: All men are rapists. I made the call from my dorm, named Mallory, the all-women/wimmin/womyn feminist collective where I lived sophomore year. To my dad's credit, he just

listened quietly and made his excuses and got off the phone—
wondering, I'm sure, why he bothered writing tuition checks.

Even though it's fun to mock Oberlin and the dopey abso-
lutism of my statement, of course my young self was right to
rail against what kept happening to her. In very real ways, I
was in fact a victim. And so we must once again do like old
F. Scott Fitzgerald and try to hold opposing ideas in our teeny
brains, both at the same time. Two facts, in conflict and simultaneously true. I can be excited by the idea of victimhood and
still have been victimized. Even if I've turned into grist for the
sexual mill, nonetheless, I didn't get to *choose* to be victimized
that first time, that first among many. I didn't get to choose the
historical circumstances that have complicated my life. I get to
own and even enjoy my excitement over being dominated or
punished, but I also get to be pissed at a culture that didn't protect me.

And, perhaps most terrifying, most humiliating—most
exciting?—of all: Whether I like it or not, as I grow older and
lose my beauty, I also lose the opportunity to be victimized in
the particular way I crave and fear.

May 11, 1984, age seventeen

I don't feel great about men right now.

22

Dear Roman Polanski, Part Deux

Dear Roman Polanski,

I'm back! I'll never stop thinking about you, RP. You can sleep like a baby at night, knowing that.

I've been thinking of you as I drive my daughter back and forth to school, along the island roads lined with Douglas firs and scooping-branched cedars. I drive her and I keep her safe. At least I think she's safe. I'm a mother who, like my contemporaries, will mostly usually choose safety in the ongoing battle between safety and freedom. Her sexuality, her femininity— these burgeoning qualities are to be protected at any cost, even as my own diminish: I feel like a troll whose job is not to menace the heroine but to drive her to piano practice.

I try hard to protect my girl. Did Samantha's mother do the same? Much has been written and said about Mrs. Gailey—most especially by your own apologists, who are legion—that she and Samantha were opportunists, that she was a bad mother. Surely she must have been very bad indeed to have allowed this to happen. That is how the thinking goes.

What happened was this: The mother allowed the counterculture into their household, and the daughter paid the price. If we blame the mother, are we saying that opening the door in the first place was wrong, a bad idea? Are we prepared to hoist all the baggage that comes with such a position—all the liberties that we'd have to roll back? Should the grown-ups have refused the counterculture and its freedoms?

Some people believe that's exactly what should've been done. For instance, the people who blamed you for Sharon Tate's death. Martin Amis wrote in 1979: "[Polanski's] period of recovery [from Tate's murder] was then marked by constant, and hatefully insulting, stories in the press, explaining how Mr and Mrs Polanski had opened the door to their own nemesis (by experimenting with drugs, decadence, weird rituals, etc.)." It seems ridiculous to say that freedom is wrong. As a mother, I try hard not to say this. I try to protect my children but also to keep their worlds expanding all the time. At Oberlin, I remember being part of some feminist group that was discussing freedom versus safety. Which would you want more for your children, the group leader asked, safety or freedom? Every woman in the room answered "safety" except me and one other person, who confidently answered "freedom." The two of us glanced at each other guiltily. Had there been a wrong answer? Had we just given it?

I still believe in my children's freedom. And yet. Are we willing to sacrifice our virgins to our own freedom? If we want to open our doors to the new, to the weird, to strangers who bring unprecedented ideas and ways of being, well, sometimes those new people do things we don't exactly expect. So should we stop, just because it might endanger our children? I mean, I personally as a mother would say, *Yes,* stop, please do stop, of course our children should be protected. And yet. I'm the mother on the island who lets her daughter travel freely to the city alone. Her dad and I have let her explore my old Gomorrah by Elliott Bay since she was in middle school, let her take the bus around the city by herself. I mentioned this to some other mothers at an island cocktail party and they looked at me like I was out of my gourd: Alone? In the city?

The moms think she'll get touched or snatched. And they might be right, god knows. I know. She might run into someone like *you*, Roman Polanski. So why do I let her go? Do I *want* her to be a lost soul the way I was? Am I ill-wishing her, Maleficent-like? I don't think so.

When my daughter comes home from Seattle, her hair is ferry-blown, her cheeks rosy, her eyes shining. They are eyes that have *seen things,* minus the obstructing glaucoma of a nearby parent. She has been on an adventure. She doesn't look one bit lost. She looks like the sharpest thing going.

When I talk to women my age about the 1970s, the stories spill out: not quite appropriate teachers, hot tubbing with a handsy friend of the family, a mom's boyfriend who was never quite right, and on and on. These stories are seen as no big deal, and in a certain way they're simply an intensification of a general mood or situation that we lived with all the time, an amplification of the feeling of being slightly exposed, like we were rabbits in the middle of a field, with raptors circling.

But don't all these no-big-deal moments add up to kind of a big deal?

I didn't know, when I was young, about the other girls in the night, all the other girls and the no-big-deal moments that happened to them. The girl who got felt up by an older boy on the bus on a field trip. The girl tongue-kissed repeatedly by her sister's much older boyfriend. The girl whose older brother's friend abducted her "for fun" for the afternoon and sexually molested her in the back of his family's van. The girl who made out with her youth-group leader; the girl whose breasts were felt by the camp counselor; the girl pawed by her mom's drunk boyfriend, just getting a little feel, no big deal. These are stories I know now; I didn't know them then.

But you know all about this, Roman Polanski—all about the worst of men's desires. To Amis you explained the press's fascination with you thus: "I realise, if I have *killed* somebody, it wouldn't have had so much appeal to the press you see? But . . . fucking, you see, and the young girls. Judges want to fuck young girls. Juries want to fuck young girls—*everyone* wants to fuck young girls!" And it turns out you were right, not to mention legion: All across the dark nights of the 1970s, there were men doing things to girls. Would it have helped if I'd known this at the time?

All I know is I don't want any of this to happen to my daughter. I can't keep the world and its busy hands off of her forever, but maybe she's made it this far. Maybe she's been safe.

She *seems* like a person who's safe; in fact, she seems like a person who is utterly secure. When she turned thirteen, Roman Polanski, you appeared in my brain out of nowhere, on my daughter's birthday, like the bad fairy Blackstick. I was worried about her thirteenth birthday, though I didn't want to think about it. It was too hard to think about. So instead I thought about Samantha Gailey, and I got mad at you.

You, Roman Polanski, became my very own monster of sexuality, and I loathed you, at a very high word count. I started this letter years ago, and then I just kept writing it. But really I was writing to the world: Please don't hurt my daughter. Please let her be both safe *and* free.

I look at her and I think . . . it might have worked. She might be both, safe and free, in a way I never was. My daughter is a poised cat with a beautiful, rare giggle and a complex and *very* well protected interior life. Not protected in a rigid, rampart-y way but protected the way a nature preserve is protected. That's what her introversion is like: a wisely and beautifully maintained defense of a wild place.

We own, with some friends, a little cabin north of Seattle; it's in the San Juan Islands, not far from the remote island where I grew up, where the Jack Wolf thing happened. I love those islands. Part of the reason I fell in love with my husband was the fact that he and a pal owned that piece of land, even though he lived in a shitty studio apartment. We hung on to the land, and eventually with a group of friends built a tiny mouse-infested cabin there. Some lucky summers, if I organize my freelancing cleverly, I end up there with the kids for weeks on end. When we arrive, Lucy and her dad put up her tent. They secure the rain fly. She adds a mattress, a stack of books. We run an electrical cord out from the house to power a little lantern. And off she goes, for the month, to live outside like a free girl. Bruce and Willie and I stay in the house, reading ourselves to sleep in our loft each night in a state of blissful togetherness; Lucy, meanwhile, is alone on the hillside above us. Throughout the night, she climbs in and out of her tent so she can look at the falling Perseid. She's not afraid.

Four years have passed, to the week, since I started writing this letter. It's another August day, another writing day, and once again I'm sitting at a large desk, eating cookies, and writing about *you*. This time I'm not about to lose my shit; I lost it already. I lost it and lost it and lost it. I lay in bed for a year; I cried for two. I got kissed or just chatted up or occasionally groped by men not my husband (note use of passive voice) and wrote them letters and had long phone chats with them. I blew deadlines. I forgot appointments for my kids. I fell down on the job in every conceivable way: as a mother, a wife, a writer, a friend. I received furious or, worse, *concerned* e-mails from almost everyone I knew. I *fucked up*. I learned that I'm still the person I was all those years ago, when I was a girl.

I don't think I'll ever really be better. I'll always wish I was a dude. I'll always be a flirt. What was that thing I wrote in my diary? "Completely allied with masculinity—that unbelievably beautiful feeling of 'I shouldn't be here, I'm here' that I get whenever I am around some testosterone." Male attention will always be of value to me. I'll always feel embarrassed by my sexuality and completely at its mercy. People don't change. Which is maybe bad news for you and me, RP, but good news when it comes to having a daughter like *that*.

'Til next time . . .

October 12, 1990, age twenty-three

I don't think I'm built to last.

23

Consolations and Desolations

In the rainy-ass winter of 2015, Victoria and I decided we wanted to go to Utah to see the earthwork *Spiral Jetty*. The jetty was built in 1970 by the artist Robert Smithson on the shore of the Great Salt Lake. Constructed of giant boulders by a team of bulldozer-driving men, the thing extended into the lake. Visitors walked its furl and found themselves out on the water. But then the lake rose, and the piece was submerged for three decades. It reappeared in 2002, and now *Spiral Jetty* fluctuated in its visibility. When the lake was high, it disappeared; in drought times, it reappeared. Drought conditions bared the jetty this year, and Vic and I were determined to see it for ourselves. We wanted to look at this emerging and disappearing structure, which seemed ridiculously metaphorical. Or maybe we just liked to walk around things. We were both as sad as ever, but making elaborate travel plans was a kind of bulwark against the sadness. Anyway, it was as good as we could muster. Vic seemed genuinely thrilled. I was buffeted by her intention. That was all I wanted: to have a thing to do, a feint against death.

We planned our trip for June, when the high desert would be neither too hot nor too cold.

A week before I was slated to leave, I got the flu. "Maybe I shouldn't go," I said, feeling daunted and exhausted. "Are you fucking crazy?" Bruce said. "It's gonna be awesome. Go." It struck me this was an ongoing conversation of our marriage.

We flew into Salt Lake City at the crack of dawn, giddy with lack of sleep. Below us the massive scale of the lake and the plains and the mountains conspired to make the landscape unintelligible. Miles and miles of bog and sand flowed past, uninterrupted by any landmark; distances were unguessable. When a house did appear, it looked even smaller than houses usually look from an airplane. I poked Vic and she removed her earbuds. I pointed out the window and whispered, "Tiny bog Mormons!"

I was obsessed with Mormons. Every time I went to SLC all I could do was assess everyone for Mormon-ness and conjecture about their underwear. Also, I had a slightly offensive prejudice that all Mormons were, well, rapists. This was because of the marrying twelve-year-olds biz. There had been a period when I wouldn't even drive through Salt Lake City because I was so badly upset by the idea of these twelve-year-old girls. We had to drive around, which was no easy task, what with the Wasatch mountains and all. Now I just joked compulsively, bitterly.

We spent the day looking at Mormons and their edifices. I made jokes about rape the whole time; Vic endured it. Then we departed Salt Lake City and officially began our expedition. We would mount our attack on the jetty from the enchantingly named Crystal Inn Hotel in Brigham City. We went to bed at midnight. Vic pottered leggy in her underpants around the hotel room, preparing her cameras and tripods. I thought about why I loved her: She never fucking stopped. She wanted to make a time-lapse series about the jetty, capturing it as the light changed, and I mused half asleep that she had a time-lapse brain, it click-clicked on and on.

Next morning we were up at three fifteen. Vic wanted to photograph the jetty at sunrise, matins. We headed out into the black desert. Before too long we left the pavement behind and barreled along a maze of dirt roads, swilling coffee and beer alternately, swerving to avoid the throngs of bunnies who moronically zigzagged across our headlights ("Serpentine! Serpentine!"). Our only driving directions, involving a lot of cattle gates, were downloaded from the website of the Dia Art Foundation, which maintained the jetty—indeed, owned it, though it was odd to think of the jetty being owned.

When we arrived at *Spiral Jetty* at four forty-five, we could barely make out its shape in the nautical twilight. The lake had retreated beyond visibility, at least in the dawn gloaming; the jetty was high and dry, a dark kink of boulders on sand. Vic immediately busied herself setting up a time-lapse camera while I stood there in a halo of mosquitoes, my hood pulled tight over my face, feeling stunned and dumb. Once Vic's camera was in place, we walked the curling length of the thing itself, which in the dark seemed mostly like a Mormon bug resort. We separated and came together, didn't talk very much because I was preverbal.

Now that I was here, I wasn't sure I understood *Spiral Jetty* at all. Vic, on the other hand, was thinking hard about the jetty. She wasn't talking, but I could tell by looking at her that she was having Thoughts. She had that stubborn faith that it meant something—another thing I loved about her: She believed everything meant something. Though of course mostly I loved her because she laughed at all my jokes.

As the sun rose, we stepped off the jetty and headed out over the flats toward the lake's edge. We found ourselves in the girliest, most princessy landscape ever: The water was pink with algae bloom; the sunrise was pink; the flats were salt-whitened, so they reflected the pink sky. We were in an entirely pink world, with no visible distinction between land, water, sky. We lay down on the hard salt flats and giggled helplessly, rolling around to get different views of our new pink world.

The sun finally came up and broke the cold. We separated again and roamed the flats. Vic found a pink bog and guided me to it; it was like an expanse of swampy cotton candy made entirely of crystals and algae bloom. Pink bog! we said, liking how it echoed the title of our favorite album, Wire's *Pink Flag*. Pink bog—we decided it was a new name for my vag. The whole landscape was just ridiculously feminine. To push it over the top, tiny crystals sprouted in ridge after ridge, a New Age lady's daft dream come true. I kept licking everything and it all tasted like salt. "You'll cut yourself!" said Vic, but I licked anyway. We were wandering through the desert like John the Baptist and somehow it was the silliest thing imaginable.

By eleven, we'd had the jetty and miles of pink emptiness to ourselves for six hours, with only sky things (pelicans and Cessnas) for company. Now people started showing up. We climbed the hillside above the jetty and watched the little figures come and go, all ant-like.

From up there, you could see the spiral perfectly, see the people walking it. They came around again and again to a place that was the same but a little different.

I read a study about women in West Africa. For them, aging was not quite so linear as it is for us. The women past child-bearing age found themselves in a renewed, glowing state; they were described by the same word that was used for virgins. A woman who found herself in such a state sometimes would say, "I am again in my twelve." I could imagine that for a woman of West Africa, being in her twelve was a fucking relief—all that exhausting, dangerous baby-having over at last. I was again in my twelve. The spiral had tightened and I returned to my former self. Or rather: I was in my twelve, and my twenty, and my forty-seven all at once. All I could do was keep going.

Keep Going was the name of our trip to *Spiral Jetty*. Keep going, around and around, and sometimes you would meet the old self, and maybe when you'd met it enough times, you might learn to stop hating it. Maybe!

I went behind a cactus to pee and was surprised by a father and daughter vrooming past on three-wheelers. The engine sounds filled the air. It was *really* time to go. Suddenly I was as cranky as a toddler. We'd been here eight hours—a full workday. The inside of my nose was thick with dry desert snot. The sun was unforgiving, like a Mormon rapist. I looked at Vic, importuning, and she sighed and said, "Okay." She could've stayed here forever.

We loaded all our stuff into the car and headed back to civilization. We would stay that night at a Park City resort where we'd drink martinis and swim in a swimming pool. But first we had to find our way out of this place, which felt like the end of the earth, which might have been the end of the earth for all we knew. The dirt roads crisscrossed each other and, exhausted, we lost track of where we were going. Vic made what I was convinced was a wrong turn and I lost my temper a little. We bickered about the route, drank the last warm beer, felt obscurely changed even though we were still the same.

Acknowledgments

This little book took more than five years to write. During that time, many kind, smart, generous people supported me in both word and deed. Some people helped with the gift of the right conversation at the right moment; some helped with huge tranches of time and friendship and wisdom and expertise. Thank you to Suzanne Morrison, Joanna Rakoff, Peter Mountford, Hedgebrook, Margot Page, Erika Schickel, Hugo House, Jarret Middleton, Hanna Rosin, Tom Nissley, Peggy Orenstein, Theo Pauline Nestor, Courtney Hodell, Dani Shapiro, Steve Fradkin, Linda Mangel, David Shields, Harriet Phinney, Rebecca Rockefeller, Maria Semple, Dave Lipe, Tia Matthies, Pat Riley, Ann Hulbert, James Marcus, Jeanne Garland, Jeff Garland, Anne Phyfe Palmer, Bez Palmer, Heidi Thorsen, Johnny Stutsman, Chris Thorsen, Diana Roll, Scott Loveless, Teresa Howard, Mike Dederer, Dave Dederer, Donna Dederer, Larry Jay, Jessica Purcell, Paul Bogaards, Nicholas Thomson, all my students. Ed Fotheringham, for the map. Deepest gratitude to Jordan Pavlin, my ideal reader. Don't ever leave me, Anna Stein.

I have always regretted not acknowledging my children's babysitters and nannies in my first book—the omission seems to me a failure of my own feminism. So thank you to Joelle Berry, Anna Morris Keltz, and Molly MacGuffie for helping me remain a writer through those childbearing years.

For just everything, that's all: Victoria Haven. I know you know.

My family, the great love: Bruce, Lucy, Willie.